THE
ACCIDENTAL
FUNDRAISER

THE ACCIDENTAL FUNDRAISER

Second Edition

A Step-by-Step Guide to Raising Money for Your Cause

HALEY BASH • STEPHANIE ROTH

ISBN: 9798992147803 (print)
ISBN: 9798992147810 (epub)

Library of Congress Control Number: 2025911905

First printing Summer 2025

Design and book production by Happenstance Type-O-Rama
Front cover image © Nazarevich | iStockPhoto

TABLE OF CONTENTS

Selling

PREFACE

Fundraising is like one of those words you've never heard of and then once you do, you find that it's everywhere. As people who raise money (and help others do so as well) for a living, we knew that many in our circles were not always all that interested in hearing much about it. But when we talked to them about causes near and dear to them—like getting money to people who couldn't afford an abortion, or to communities suffering in the aftermath of a devastating fire, or even to support their kid's school's music program—we started hearing story after story about something they or someone they knew had done to raise money for a cause.

Hearing their stories, and also hearing that there weren't many resources out there that provided truly useful how-to fundraising information that wasn't aimed at established nonprofits, convinced us that a book like this could be helpful to the large numbers of people who want to support something they care about.

Fundraising has become commonplace in the United States, in part because so many public institutions (schools, libraries, parks) that had been completely supported by taxes are facing budget cuts as the government has abdicated responsibility for meeting even the most basic of community needs. The result is that more and more programs that were supported by our tax dollars are now seeking financial help from individuals, local businesses, and private foundations. That means more and more of you are being asked to help raise that money.

On a more positive note, people are also raising money because they are moved by a pressing community need, by a desire to make a difference in the world, or just to come together with their neighbors to improve the conditions in which they live. They decide they want to do something: organize a local theater group, clean up a toxic site in the neighborhood, support relief efforts in a community devastated by climate change or wars, lobby the city council for better lighting at night, get their community to provide better services to survivors of domestic violence, or provide more books and teaching materials for their local schools. In order to accomplish these projects—some of which are short-term, while others will take years to complete—they realize they need to bring people together to make it happen. They need people to participate by giving their time, and they need some of them to contribute money as well.

This book was not written for professional fundraisers, though if you fall into that category you may find some ideas here that you haven't tried before and some that will likely be helpful to your volunteer team. It was not written for people working in nonprofit organizations who need to create the systems, infrastructure, and technology required to carry out sophisticated fundraising programs on an ongoing basis. This book was written for anyone who finds themselves unexpectedly needing to raise some money to carry out a particular project, activity, or event. It might be a time-specific need, such as attending a conference, supporting emergency relief efforts, or building a community center. Or it might be something that starts out as a one-time effort and then grows into an ongoing activity because you find yourself thrilled with what you were able to accomplish.

You might be a political activist or a member of a community organization, and while you never thought that raising money was something you'd do, you finally agree at least to help out.

Or maybe you're a board member of a nonprofit organization and have learned that board members are expected to help raise money. If you don't really know where to start, this book can help steer you in the right direction.

The fundraising strategies described here are ones that a small team of people can organize and carry out, whether you're brand new to fundraising or someone with experience who wants to take your efforts to the next level.

HOW TO GET THE MOST OUT OF THIS BOOK

If your fundraising goal is less than $3,000, you can probably use any one of the strategies described in the following chapters. If you need to raise a larger amount, you will most likely use a few different strategies over a period of several months or a year.

The fundraising strategies described in this book are organized into three major categories or approaches: **Direct Asks** (Chapters 6 and 7); **Gatherings** (Chapters 8–10); and **Selling** (Chapters 11–14).

We assume that most of you will be carrying out these activities as a volunteer, including those of you who serve on boards of nonprofits where fundraising is one of your responsibilities. Or you may be a paid staffer for a small organization, or from an organization with limited resources. For these reasons, we've provided as much detailed how-to information as possible, with worksheets and forms you can adapt for your particular situation and with an approach that keeps the process as simple and manageable as possible for anyone doing these activities in their spare time.

Each chapter in Part II, Fundraising Strategies, begins with a discussion of the best uses of that strategy and things to consider in deciding whether it's a good strategy for your group to take on. Next, there is a summary list of steps for carrying out the strategy, followed by a detailed discussion of each step. The steps for each strategy are quite similar and generally consist of the following:

1. Make a plan.

2. Recruit, train, and orient volunteers.

3. Prepare materials (and/or find a location).

4. Create lists of people to ask.

5. Start asking and/or publicizing.

6. Track contacts made and donations received.

7. Send regular updates and follow up with your volunteer team.

8. Do final preparations as needed.

9. Carry out the activity.

10. Evaluate the activity and thank people.

Each strategy chapter has an associated sample workplan online that provides a spreadsheet template of these key tasks and a proposed timeline for implementation. The workplans give you a quick and easy way to see the order in which tasks should be completed and approximately how long each should take. Use these workplans as guides from which to develop your own plan and timeline.

For some strategies, you'll need to find out about any special legal requirements or restrictions that may apply. For example, with car washes, you can run into problems if you don't dispose of the wastewater properly. Such special considerations are discussed in the relevant chapter.

Each strategy in this book will work better under some circumstances than others. Some are better if you have lots of volunteers available to help out, even if what they're willing to do is limited (selling raffle tickets or donating items for a garage sale or an auction, for example). Other strategies are better if you have lots of people you could ask to support your cause (e.g., phonebanks or personal asks). And still others are better if you have a group of people who like to socialize (such as community events or house parties). In any case, we have only included fundraising strategies that we know many groups of all sizes have had success with using a volunteer team.

Another element that varies by strategy is how important potential donors' motivation is, such as whether they care deeply about your cause or are willing to give because of their relationship with you. For a car wash, factors such as a dirty car, convenient location, and timing might be just as important to someone as the fact that you have a cause they want to support. For someone to agree to make a small contribution in response to your email appeal or phone call, it will be more important that they support the cause or your efforts to raise money. For someone to make a large contribution, they will need to have a deeper belief in the cause or trust that you, the asker, are raising money for something important.

Whatever activity you choose, you'll be most successful if you can get others to help you carry it out. Even when a strategy doesn't make the most sense to you based on your consideration of various factors, if it's the one your volunteer team is most excited about (or just willing to do), then it may be the best choice.

For each strategy, we've included worksheets and workplans to help you organize your fundraising efforts. You can find these worksheets and workplans in spreadsheet form for copying and downloading at *https://donororganizerhub.org/worksheets*.

Finally, we've included additional information and tips (what we've called "Resources"), starting on page 187. We put them in one section because each of them is helpful for several of the strategies. The Resources include ideas of who you can ask (to help brainstorm lists of people to include on your volunteer and fundraising lists), a form to track volunteer recruitment, ideas for raffle and auction items and prizes to seek out, and more.

Although you might be tempted to go right to the chapter that describes a fundraising activity you'd like to try out, we recommend that you read the chapters in Part I first to better understand fundamentals of successful fundraising. You'll be glad you did.

PART I

Fundraising Basics

Part I is useful to read before you choose a fundraising strategy to carry out. The information in these chapters provides a context for understanding how fundraising works, the elements of successful fundraising, and how to get the most out of whatever strategy you choose. These chapters present an important reminder that fundraising isn't just about money but about building relationships, carrying out a vision, and strengthening community.

Chapter 1 discusses basic fundraising principles and tips to help you get over your fear of asking for money. Chapter 2 explains the important difference between direct and indirect asks or solicitations, and how to make the best use of each approach. In Chapter 3, you'll learn how to recruit other people to help, because you'll always raise more money and have more fun if you make fundraising a group effort. You'll also get useful tips for how to work as a team and how to deal with the challenges that arise within any group of people. Chapter 4 reminds you of a lesson you probably learned as a child—that thanking people is important. Not only is it the right thing to do, but it also tells the people who contributed to your cause that their support made a difference and increases the likelihood that they'll be willing to give again in the future. You'll also find sample thank-you letters that you can adapt for your own situation. Chapter 5 addresses the kinds of things you'll want to think about if you decide to do ongoing fundraising. These considerations include how to keep track of your donors and volunteers and how to document what you learned from your fundraising efforts so that you can revise and refine your strategy when you go back to do it again.

We hope this section will inspire and motivate you to set ambitious goals and to take the time to make a plan that is both realistic and achievable. You'll learn that you *can* raise money and that millions of people are engaged in doing just that every day.

1

You *Can* Ask for Money

You probably picked up this book because, like so many people in communities around the country, you have found yourself in the (maybe unexpected) position of needing to raise money for something, and you want to find the easiest, quickest way to do that. Like so many skills, raising money is one anyone can do, and just jumping in and trying out some new things is probably the best way to learn. But unlike reading, cooking, riding a bicycle, or using a computer, fundraising is a skill very few people are excited to learn. What's helpful to keep in mind, though, is that people generally feel very good about giving money to something they care about. Not only will this book help you feel more confident and excited about learning how to raise money, but it will also demystify the process.

Many of us have been taught from a young age that we shouldn't talk about money or mention the topic except under specifically prescribed situations (such as asking what something costs or negotiating the purchase of a large item like a house or car).

On the other hand, start talking about community-based fundraising activities—such as mutual aid efforts, dance-a-thons, and pancake breakfasts—and almost everyone has a story about something they or someone they know did to raise money. Unfortunately, this is partly because programs that used to be funded entirely by the government, and for which we pay taxes, can no longer count on sufficient funding to meet their needs, and are forced to turn to the private sector for support. This includes public schools, public parks, and even public health departments. This is also in part because, for some constituencies like queer and trans communities, government funding has always been insufficient or even nonexistent. But there are also people who are inspired to make the world a better place, are working on a controversial issue for which funding is hard to come by, and need money to fund a new idea or project toward that end. These people don't necessarily work in a nonprofit organization or consider themselves fundraisers, but they realize that fundraising will help them achieve their goals.

When you start raising money for a cause you care about, you will find that the process of asking people for money often involves raising their awareness about the issue. For example, by raising money to organize people to stop a corporation found to be dumping toxic waste into a local river, you are also educating them about the problem. When you start communicating one-on-one to your friends and neighbors, through social media, or by holding a public fundraising event, you spread the word about your cause far beyond the relatively small team of people who devote much of their time to the group's mission.

Here are some quotes from volunteer fundraisers on why they enjoy fundraising or what changed their mind about it:

When you're fundraising for something you love, you're building your community because you find other people who care about that same thing.

—JUAN GOVEA

I was taught early in my career that in order to build grassroots power, we need to bring together people and resources—and that's what a fundraiser does. Once I realized that being willing to raise money is critical to getting things done and making change, I was in. And now I've been fundraising for over twenty-five years as a volunteer, board member, and staff member.

—PRISCILLA HUNG

Asking people for money can be uncomfortable, but it also can be an opportunity to invite someone into the issue you care about. And people give because you asked them. Money is power, and movements have always mobilized money to support their efforts. I started being a volunteer fundraiser because I saw that telling my story moved other people to share why this work matters to them.

—JOSIE AHRENS

We recognize, too, that there are cultural differences in how people relate to each other and how groups function. Successful fundraising does not require that all requests for support be done in a certain way. Consider what approaches will work in your community—whether it's better to be more or less direct in your ask, more specific about a particular program or more general about your group, and so on. What's most important to understand is that there are few absolutes in fundraising. It's like many other activities that we carry out in our lives without thinking about them—we know what will offend people and what will make them feel good, what will make them feel excluded or included in a group, and what will make them want to give money to an organization that is working for something they believe in. In all cultures, people get together to effect change and raise money to do so.

WHO CAN I ASK? FUNDRAISING CBAs

At this point you may be asking yourself: *Who* can I ask to give? Fundraising CBAs (Contact, Belief, and Ability) allow you to prioritize and strategize the people you ask to donate to your cause.

C Is for Contact: Who Do You Know?

Most of the strategies described in this book require you to tap into networks of potential supporters that you already know. You'll have a much greater chance of getting a yes from someone you know than from a stranger. An exception to this is if the person you're asking has already donated to your group, and therefore knows the group, if not you personally.

When you start to come up with a list of people you might approach to ask for financial support, it can be helpful to refer to Resource B on page 188, Who Can You Ask? This resource provides some categories of people in your life—including friends, family, neighbors, colleagues, and more—to consider asking. Keep in mind that this is just the first step in generating a list and that you likely won't ask *all* of them because you'll want to look at other criteria to determine whether or not they are potential supporters. But you'll find that your list will increase substantially if you take the time to consider all of the people you know.

B Is for Belief: The People You Ask Should Care (Even a Little) About Your Cause

Even if someone is a very generous donor to many groups, their likelihood of giving to *your* cause is greater if the issue is one they care about as well. The overturning of *Roe v. Wade* in 2022, which led to a devastating increase in restrictions on abortion in many states, was followed by a surge in both activism and donations to the hundreds of abortion funds around the country that provide funding and travel support for those needing abortions.

The key takeaway in figuring out who to ask is to identify people you know who care about your issue and to prioritize those who care deeply.

A Is for Ability: Who Gives Away Money?

When you start thinking about who to ask for a donation to your group, your first thought might be, *I don't know anyone with money*. That's very common. However, we know from years of experience that what you're looking for from your list of potential supporters is those you know who *give away* money, rather than those who might *have* a lot of money. (And what is "a lot," anyway? It's a relative term.)

Studies have shown that seven out of ten Americans give away money. This includes people of all class and race backgrounds, ages, genders, and sexual orientations. That means at least some people you know (probably about 70 percent of them) already support causes they care about. Moreover, most of the people who give donate to several different organizations.

The most important thing to keep in mind is that people actually like to give money to things they care deeply about. People want to be involved in their communities and in making a positive difference in the world. And sometimes making a financial contribution is the easiest way for them to do that. In fundraising workshops we've led, when we ask participants if they feel good when they make a contribution to an organization or cause they care about, most of them raise their hands. But when we ask the same people if they feel good asking a friendly, supportive person to give money to their cause, very few people raise their hands. This tells us, not surprisingly, that people are more comfortable giving than asking.

Some people don't have time to volunteer, so their way to be involved is by giving, while people who already volunteer are more willing to give if asked since their level of commitment to the organization is already higher than that of someone who isn't involved.

The takeaway here is that if you focus your attention more on the good feelings people get from giving and less on your own discomfort with asking, you'll find asking for money a lot easier. Remember that people want to give, and if you don't ask them to support something you think they would care about, you're leaving money on the table.

How *much* to ask someone for is a different question. People's capacity to give a gift of a particular amount will vary greatly, of course, and it's important to consider the amount you think is reasonable to ask them for. There's no absolute formula for determining how much money to ask someone for. If they have donated to your group before, you can ask them to give that amount again or to consider increasing their gift. If they haven't donated previously, you can ask them for an amount within a range that is your best guess of what they might be willing to give.

In any case, we do not recommend that you ask everyone to donate the same amount (say, $20), because we know that for any given fundraising effort, people will give different amounts based on what they feel they can afford and how motivated they are by the asker or the cause itself. If you ask everyone for $20, those who can afford and are willing to give much more are likely to only give what you asked for. And those who can only afford $10 will likely not give at all. In Chapter 6, we walk through a gift range chart to help you figure out how many contributions of what amounts you'll need to reach your goal.

GETTING OVER THE FEAR OF ASKING

Kim Klein, nationally acclaimed fundraising trainer and author, writes about the psychological barriers to asking for money. We have found the following insights from her extremely useful in helping people overcome their reluctance to ask for money:

1. If you want money, you have to ask for it. *While there are some people who will simply send an organization money or offer money without being asked, most people will not think to give you money unless you make your needs known. This is not because they are cheap or self-centered; it is because most people have no idea how much it costs to run an organization or do grassroots social justice work. If you don't ask them, they will simply assume you are getting the money you need somewhere else.*

2. It has to be okay with you for people to say no. *Your job is to ask, to offer people the opportunity to give to your group. The person being asked also has a job; their job is to take you up on your offer or to turn you down. What they do will depend on their mood, their financial circumstance, their other commitments—many variables that you can't do anything about and that are not about you or your group. People who say no may say it directly: "No, I can't help you." They may say no by never responding to your calls, emails, or social media posts. They may* *say no by saying, "I'll think about it" and never get back to you. And they even may say no by saying yes and then never pay their pledge. While not paying a pledge may be a way of indirectly saying "no," you should absolutely follow up with anyone who says they will make a donation—including by phone, email and text, and more than once— before concluding that they are just not going to pay. People will sometimes lose track of their commitments, get overwhelmed or distracted by other things in their lives, and don't actually mean to disregard their pledge.*

By knowing that many people will not say yes to your request, you can feel good about having taken a chance at asking and having done your job in the fundraising effort in which you are participating. In fact, experience has shown that you can expect fewer than half the people you ask to say yes to making a donation. This means you'll need to identify two to three times as many people to ask as the number of gifts you need, and two to three times the amount of money you need as well.

3. What you believe in has to be bigger than what you are afraid of. *If you don't like asking for money, or you would rather not do it, or you wish someone else would do it for you, that is normal. That is how most people are. But we suggest you think about what will happen if you don't ask anyone for money. What will happen to your cause or project? Does it matter if you're unable to raise the money you need? If it matters to you, then put that first, ahead of your anxiety about asking. There is an old fundraising saying, "If you are afraid to ask for money, kick yourself out of the way and let the cause talk."*

4. You will need to ask some people, but you don't need to ask everyone. *Many people never get out of the starting gate because they think they have to ask everyone they know. Don't ask people you have a difficult relationship with or who don't believe in your cause. Start with someone very easy: yourself. When you go to ask someone to donate, you want to be able to say, "Join me in supporting this important cause." If you're not willing to give, how can you expect anyone else to? Make your own gift first, and one that is significant for you—that you feel it and it feels good. Then go to friends and family members whom you like, who like you, and who agree with the cause you represent.*

5. Put yourself in the donor's shoes. *You may not like asking, but that doesn't mean the donor doesn't want to be asked. Most people like to be seen as helpful and generous. They like to be included. And many people give because they are affected by the issue directly and want to be a part of the solution by giving. Sometimes organizations go out of* *business and people around them will say, "I never knew they were in trouble. Why didn't they ask for help?" There are far more hurt feelings from not being included and not being asked than there ever will be from being asked.*

MAKING YOUR CASE FOR SUPPORT

Before you start asking people you know for money or to join you in asking others for money, you need to be able to make a case for why people should give to your cause. Often we get so involved in an issue or project, we forget that other people don't necessarily understand the importance, urgency, or even the impact of the issue we're working on. We lapse into jargon or phrases that only those of us working closely on the project really understand.

So along with coming up with a solid plan, clearly defined tasks, and a group of people willing to carry them out, you also need to describe what you're raising money for in a way that draws the attention and interest of potential donors. Put yourself in their shoes as you imagine making a pitch to them. What would move you to respond favorably to a request? What would stand out in your mind about what that person said?

As you draft your case for support, reflect on the following:

- Why this issue matters (including to you, the asker, and to the person you're asking)

- Why you asked them (what they believe in or care about)

- Why you need the money now

Most important in coming up with a message is that it's brief—you can say it in two or three sentences—and that rather than answering "What does your group do?" it answers two other questions: "Why is this work important or necessary?" and "How can I help?" Here are a few examples:

- **For a community health fair:** "We believe that healthy communities matter, that people need access to better resources, and that the quality of our air, land, and water are part of what makes a community healthy. We're planning a health fair to provide a range of information about resources for making our lives and the life of our community stronger and healthier. We hope you'll support this event with a contribution."

- **For a community arts project:** "We believe that everyone has artistic ability. Photography is a great place to start and a way for kids to explore their innate creativity. Will you support us in launching a photography project for kids?"

- **To enable a member of an environmental justice project to attend a national conference:** "As the toxins dumped by local industry in our town's landfill are affecting the water quality in our predominantly Black community, we are starting to fight back. Can you help us send some of our most active community members to a national conference that is working to build a grassroots response to industrial pollution?"

CHOOSING THE RIGHT STRATEGY

In deciding which of the fundraising strategies described in this book is the right one for you, you'll want to consider several things aside from the interest of volunteers. These considerations include how much lead time you have to organize the activity, how many people you can recruit to help out, how much money you need to raise, and how many people you can find to ask.

The Fundraising Strategy Grid that follows gives you a brief overview of what to expect from each strategy to help you choose the one(s) you may want to carry out. Keep in mind that the ranges given for lead time, number of volunteers needed, and so on are estimates of what is reasonable to expect. Each strategy can be used to raise more money than we've indicated here, but it may also raise less. Make sure to read through the chapter that describes the strategy you're interested in to get a better sense of what it takes to be successful at raising the money you need.

In addition to the specific fundraising strategies that make up the bulk of this book, Chapter 2 focuses on types of fundraising asks, Chapter 3 is devoted to getting others to join your fundraising efforts, Chapter 4 discusses the importance of thanking volunteers and donors, and Chapter 5 gives tips for creating longer term or ongoing fundraising programs.

FUNDRAISING STRATEGY GRID

STRATEGY	LEAD TIME	AMOUNT THAT CAN GENERALLY BE RAISED (NET)	NUMBER OF VOLUNTEERS NEEDED	NUMBER OF PEOPLE TO ASK	RESPONSE RATE[1]
Personal ask	2–6 weeks	$500–10,000 (or more!)	1–5	10–200	40–50%
Phonebank	6–8 weeks	$500–2,500	5	200–400	5–10%
House party	4–6 weeks	$500–5,000	1–2	50–100	30%
Community event	3–6 months	$1,000–5,000	10–15	200	20%
Pledge-raising event	8–10 weeks	$1,000–5,000	7–10	100–300	20–40%
Auction	3–4 months	$250–3,000	10–15	200	20%
Raffle	10–12 weeks	$500–1,000	20	400	50%
Selling goods	6–8 weeks	$300–1,500	3–10	Busy street	N/A
Selling services	3–6 weeks	$400–500	5–8	Busy street (for a car wash)	N/A

1 This is the percentage of all the people you ask who will respond with a contribution. These percentages are based on the assumption that you're making a direct ask (rather than posting a request on social media, for example).

MAKING YOUR FUNDRAISING SUCCESSFUL

Each fundraising strategy in this book has its pros and cons—elements that make it better for some communities or situations than others. As you skim through the chapters to decide which strategies you want to try, paying attention to the following common features will help you successfully raise money:

FIND A TEAM OF PEOPLE TO PARTICIPATE IN THE FUNDRAISING ACTIVITY. It can be a small team—three is what we recommend as the minimum, and more is better, depending on what your goal is and which strategy you decide to use. Working with a team will allow you to raise more money, expand the network of contacts who will ultimately lead you to more gifts, and have more fun.

SET A GOAL AND CREATE A PLAN. Different strategies require different amounts of lead time. Make sure you have enough time to carry out the tasks that will produce a successful outcome. A plan will give you the confidence that the goal you're trying to reach is realistic (even if also ambitious). Each strategy in this book includes a sample workplan and timeline at the end of the chapter describing it so you can see exactly what's involved and the kind of time you'll need.

IDENTIFY ONE OR TWO PEOPLE TO ORGANIZE THE WORK. You may have a team of the most responsible and reliable people helping out, but having one or two people who keep on top of the details, stay in touch with everyone on the team, and encourage team members will make all the difference.

Another important task for the organizer(s) is to keep track of donations made and any follow-up required with either the team members or donors.

BE SURE TO THANK EVERYONE INVOLVED. Remember to include your volunteers as well as the people who donate money. Thanking people isn't just the right thing to do, it will make it possible for you to go back to volunteers and donors in the future and ask them to help again.

KEEP IN MIND THAT FUNDRAISING IS REALLY ABOUT RELATIONSHIPS. Even if you plan to do this only as a "one-time" activity, how you relate to everyone you work with will matter. Keeping relationships in mind means helping make the experience of volunteering, asking for money, and donating to your cause a positive one so that people feel good about the experience and your group. This will help them remain open to being involved with other causes in the future.

IN-KIND CONTRIBUTIONS

Often what you need most, either to help a fundraising activity bring in more money or in place of a monetary gift, is a donation of a service, a facility, or goods from a small business or larger corporation. Some projects depend almost entirely on a combination of time from volunteers and items or services from businesses, unions, and nonprofits, with very little cash exchanged.

Many of the strategies described in this book count on at least some of the support to come from these *in-kind contributions*. They may include raffle prizes; auction items; office space to do a phonebank; a community center or parking lot to hold a garage sale or other event; printing and photocopying services; design services for your invitations, flyers, and website; and food and drink for various events.

As you're putting together your budget, include in-kind contributions wherever possible. You also need to have a backup plan for the possibility that you'll have to pay for something you'd hoped would be donated.

People usually find it easier to ask for an in-kind donation than to ask for money. Identify volunteers who are more reluctant to ask for money and find out if they would be willing instead to solicit in-kind donations.

With this background in mind, you're ready to find the fundraising strategy that fits best with what you're trying to accomplish and who you can recruit to participate in the project. Go for it, and trust in yourself and your ability to do this!

2

Types of Asks

While fundraising is made up of a wide range of activities, from writing compelling messages to organizing an event to getting the word out about your cause, the one constant for any successful fundraising campaign or project is *asking*. You might be asking someone for a donation, for their time, to spread the word to their friends, or to attend a fundraising event. In general, there are two types of asks we can make: indirect asks and direct asks. Direct asks can be subdivided into two types: personal one-on-one or to a few or many people at an event.

An *indirect ask* is a mass communication ask. Indirect asks are usually made via email or print newsletters, social media, or even traditional media such as a PSA (public service announcement) on a local radio station. This type of ask is a good way to get the word out about your group and why you're raising money, but it doesn't get the same response as a more direct (and personalized) one. Keep in mind that the most common response in fundraising is no and that you have to ask many more people to donate than the number of gifts you need to reach your goal. For indirect strategies, you might solicit two thousand people on your email list and receive just one contribution in return.

By contrast, a *direct ask* solicits someone directly—and often one-on-one. A direct *personal* ask (meaning you know the person) increases the chance that the prospective donor will make a gift (of any amount) and also that they'll make a larger gift than they might have made after seeing a video on social media, for example. A personalized email that contains content written specifically to the prospective donor (e.g., "loved seeing your daughter perform in her school play last week") is a direct ask. If you are seeking a large gift, we recommend meeting with a prospect in person, on the phone, or virtually. At an event, a fundraising pitch that makes a compelling case for supporting a cause, and asks people to take immediate action by making a donation, is a form of a direct ask, although not as personal as a one-on-one appeal. A direct ask could also be a call, text, or voice memo, although the chances of a gift resulting from such an ask will greatly increase if the prospect personally knows the solicitor.

In your fundraising efforts, it can be tempting to stick to less personal, mass appeals when soliciting donations or recruiting volunteers. It's normal to feel nervous about making the people you're asking feel uncomfortable, and indirect, mass solicitations allow the recipient to ignore or reject the request by just not responding to the message.

However, if you're using both direct and indirect asks, you can expect around 80 percent of your yeses to come from direct asks. You will reach more people with mass solicitation, but you will get more, and often larger, gifts and time commitments from direct solicitation. Here are our recommendations about whether and when to make direct versus indirect appeals:

- If you want to be as successful as possible in building a team and raising the funds needed for your cause, we encourage you to make personal one-on-one asks. If you have an existing list of supporters, prioritize and assign outreach based on who your team members already have relationships with.

- If you want as many people as possible to learn about your cause, then use mass, indirect, and inherently less personal strategies. As people become more familiar with a cause, they are more likely to donate (assuming they agree with you). Marketing research has shown that people need to hear about a new product as many as seven times before they're willing to purchase it, and the same can apply to fundraising for an organization that a prospective donor may not have heard of before.

- If you've been making indirect, and less personal, asks of people in your community and haven't gotten much response, try asking them again—directly this time!

- Finally, we're not saying to never make asks in email newsletters or social media. In fact, we recommend including an ask in most of your newsletters as a way to reinforce the point that your cause needs money to carry out your work, although these kinds of asks do not tend to bring in gifts on their own. Some people who aren't on your list to contact directly *will* give or take action after seeing what you've shared through mass communication because they're passionate about the cause or they've been looking for more ways to donate or volunteer. We encourage you to incorporate mass appeals after you've tapped your networks with personal asks, or, when possible, do both at the same time.

Each of the strategies mentioned in this book involves a combination of direct, personal asks and broader, mass appeals. Being clear about what you're trying to accomplish, what you have the capacity to do, and what kind of team you have or can build to expand your reach will help you choose and carry out the best fundraising strategies for your needs.

3

Building Your Fundraising Team

All of the strategies described in this book will raise more money as you involve more people. This chapter describes the process of creating and building a successful fundraising team. By working with some basic principles of team building, you'll be able to recruit people to your fundraising campaign, make the experience a positive one for everyone, and even leave people looking forward to their next opportunity to work together. While few people would say they love to ask for money, it's possible to make fundraising fun, and paying attention to the needs of your fundraising team will make all the difference.

RECRUITING PEOPLE TO YOUR FUNDRAISING TEAM

People volunteer for different reasons:

- They believe strongly in something and want to help.

- They want to be part of a group, especially one in which people they like and respect are involved.

- They want to support the person who asks them to join.

- They like to feel needed.

- They want to contribute a skill they know would be helpful to the cause.

WHEN INVITING PEOPLE TO JOIN, THINK ABOUT WHO THEY ARE AND WHAT MOTI-VATES THEM. If you know that you're talking to someone who loves a party and the social aspect of any activity, tell them who else you're inviting to participate in this fundraising project and the opportunities they'll have to engage with the group. If you're recruiting someone who likes to feel needed, make sure they know their participation would make a difference and how much it would mean to you to have them involved. With someone who believes strongly in the issue you're raising money for, talk about the importance of the cause. In any case, don't just send a newsletter or post a request on social media and wait for people to sign up to volunteer. Actively reach out to people and make the recruitment process as personal as possible. Once you have a few volunteers, let others know who is on the team. People will be more likely to join if others they like and respect have already done so.

Finally, in addition to identifying potential volunteers based on the motivations just described, you'll want to find people who are reliable—that is, who can be counted on to follow through on their commitments. It can be demoralizing to the rest of the team when others don't show up as promised.

FIND THE RIGHT BALANCE BETWEEN DECIDING EVERYTHING ABOUT THE PROJECT AHEAD OF TIME AND BRINGING PEOPLE TOGETHER WITH THE QUESTION, *WHAT SHOULD WE DO?* If you've already decided what fundraising strategy you'll use, don't mislead your recruits into thinking they will be involved in developing new ideas. If you're starting completely from scratch, on the other hand, let potential team members know that you want their assistance in brainstorming and deciding on a project. What tends to work best is to start somewhere between these two options. Your team members will be more engaged if they are given the opportunity to help think through what the fundraising activity will be. But if the process is too open-ended, they may come up with something you think is a bad idea, and you'll be stuck trying to figure out how to get them to move to something else without alienating them in the process.

You might want to recruit a few people (say three to five) to do the initial brainstorm, where you decide between a series of house parties, a garage sale, and a silent auction, for example, and then bring in a larger team to implement and refine the activity further.

BE CLEAR ABOUT HOW MUCH TIME YOU'RE ASKING VOLUNTEERS TO COMMIT TO. If you want someone to sell raffle tickets, suggest how many you'd like them to sell. They can always say, "I can't sell that many, but I'll sell fewer." If you want a several-month commitment to organize an evening of jazz performed by local artists that also includes mounting a silent auction, your team of volunteers needs to know what they're getting themselves into.

Resource A on page 187, the Volunteer Recruitment Form, can help you identify potential volunteers for your fundraising project. Use it to help brainstorm a list of potential candidates, then think about what you're asking them to do. Carefully planning your recruitment process will help you put together a strong and enthusiastic team.

WORKING WITH A TEAM

Even if your activity doesn't require lots of meetings (which will make some people very happy), start with at least one face-to-face gathering (in person or virtual). This will start the process of relationship building that will ultimately help people work together more smoothly and make the experience a positive one.

Once you've settled on what the fundraising activity will be, the team will need to come up with a plan, timeline, and who is responsible for what specific tasks. Each strategy outlined in this book provides instructions that will help you create a realistic timeline and tell you how many people you need to carry out the strategy successfully. The timeline and the set of tasks within it are important because they help make the activity as successful as possible in reaching its goal and give team members a clear picture of what it will take so they can see how they may want to be involved.

Once the plan is complete, give the team members an opportunity to indicate how they want to help. Make sure they understand what kind of time commitment they're making and what the important deadlines are. This level of structure and detail is important with volunteers. Most people have many commitments that they need to stay on top of—job, family, and household responsibilities as well as other organizations or community projects they may be involved in. When team members are completely clear about what they've agreed to do for your fundraising project, it's much easier for them to be successful and for you to hold them accountable to that agreement.

An important step at the outset is finding out if the team needs any training on tasks they'll be working on. For example, if asking for money is something new or scary to team members, give them some training and coaching on how to do it. Soliciting auction items or prizes for a raffle may also be something people haven't done before, so give them some helpful how-tos and support them as they venture into the great unknown. At this session, which should take about two hours, volunteers should have a chance to talk about any anxieties they have about asking for money, learn some skills to make them more comfortable doing so, and complete their lists of people they will ask. Use the Sample Agenda on the following page for a Two-Hour Orientation and Training Session as a template.

SAMPLE AGENDA
for a Two-Hour Orientation and Training Session

❏ Welcome and introductions—people share why they've agreed to participate in this fundraising project.

❏ Discuss the goals and process of the fundraising: how much money you want to raise, what the money is for, and what the best strategies might be. Here's where you can solicit input from the group about what kind of activity they want to participate in.

❏ Have a discussion about people's anxieties about asking for money (or in-kind gifts). Explain that a lot of people are reluctant to ask but that most people give money away to causes they care about and that, by asking them for money, you're giving them the opportunity to be part of this exciting project, cause, or issue.

❏ Do a brief presentation on the process of asking, whether for money, for an in-kind contribution for a raffle or auction, or to invite someone to attend a community fundraiser.

❏ Role-play so that people can practice asking.

❏ Put together lists of people to ask.

❏ Discuss next steps and wrap up meeting.

TIPS ON BUILDING A STRONG FUNDRAISING TEAM

There are several things you can do to help build a strong and enthusiastic fundraising team:

- Provide material support (background on what you're raising money for, phone scripts, sample texts/emails/social media posts that team members can adapt in their own words, and so forth).

- Be a cheerleader and provide encouragement, even if you too are feeling nervous.

- Show appreciation and be open to listening to any concerns they have.

- If you're following up with someone who hasn't done what they said they would, be as specific as possible in your interactions with them. For example, rather than saying, "What's going on? I haven't heard from you in a while," say, "At the last meeting, you agreed to talk to five merchants on Main Street. I was wondering if you'd had a chance to do that yet."

- Allocate time during meetings for the team members to discuss how things are going and to give and get feedback from each other. Because things happen that you can't anticipate, you may need to make changes along the way. Explain that the group needs a certain amount of flexibility to function well.

- Provide opportunities for team members to develop relationships with each other. While some people are perfectly happy to take on a task they can do completely on their own at whatever time is best for them, many people want to be part of a group and to have some fun while doing something productive and impactful. For some suggestions, see Ideas for Making Fundraising Fun for Your Team.

- Don't let all the work fall to one or two people. This leads to resentment and burnout for those doing the work, and accusations of "control freak" and "know-it-all" from those who aren't. (If all the work is on one or two sets of shoulders, some people aren't doing their share and others are willing to do more than their share.) Often people decline to take on a task because they don't feel confident in how to do it. Always explain briefly what is involved in each task and how it connects to your fundraising goals. Offer to help or walk the person through the steps ahead of time or pair them up with a buddy. And keep in mind the tried-and-true community organizing ethos: "Never do for someone what they can do for themselves."

- Don't keep people on the committee who aren't doing anything. If you do everything recommended here and you still have people who aren't active, take them aside privately and describe to them what they haven't done. "Sarah, you haven't taken on any tasks so far. Are there tasks you would like to do?" If Sarah says, "I plan to be involved in asking local businesses for raffle items," or "I thought I could be most useful in making follow-up calls," that's great; she clearly has a specific plan. However, if she says something like, "I've just been so busy," or "My cat got an infected tooth and giving him his medicine is just taking a lot of time," then you may want to offer her an exit: "If this committee is too much work for you right now, just let me know. I don't want you to feel obligated to stay on."

- Usually a person who isn't doing their share will own up to it, and then together you can figure out whether they should stop being part of the committee or whether they have something useful to contribute. The ideal scenario is always to utilize everyone who wants to be involved.

- Use what works for you and your group. Each leader has different styles—just keep in mind the needs and styles of your group.

IDEAS FOR MAKING FUNDRAISING FUN FOR YOUR TEAM

Try some of the following:

❏ Begin each meeting by asking them to say something about why they're involved.

❏ Introduce simple icebreakers so people get to know each other better.

❏ At some meetings, bring some treats and hand each member of the team one while thanking them for something specific they've done since the last meeting.

❏ Provide food, especially if meetings take place during a mealtime.

❏ Send a quick email to people who complete their tasks: "Jody, good job with the phonebank script!"

❏ Give members of your team chances to compliment and encourage each other. Pair people up for tasks like soliciting auction items.

❏ Have each person say one thing that is going well and one thing they feel frustrated about with regard to the activity. People are often critical of themselves; this is a time to reassure everyone that you think they're doing a good job and to brainstorm with the group if a job isn't getting done.

❏ Give out silly prizes to people for various achievements: who raised the most money, got the largest number of donations, endured the worst refusal. The purpose of the prizes is to create a fun—not competitive—atmosphere. Have visuals such as thermometers or chart paper to give people a sense of their goals and accomplishments.

❏ Keep things light and fun!

GIVING FEEDBACK TO VOLUNTEERS

The time that volunteers will need the most encouragement and feedback is when they're in the process of soliciting pledges, auction items, or money for the cause. If you find that someone needs some constructive feedback on their approach to potential supporters, here's how you can do that in a way that is supportive, encouraging, and likely to be well received:

1. **Check for consent and provide rationale:** "You have an ambitious timeline for meeting your fundraising goal that requires making a certain number of asks each week. Are you okay with a quick check-in chat about this?"

2. **Name the intended outcome:** "Your goal was to send five emails or text messages each week and report back to the team leads when they were completed."

3. **Share the actual outcome:** "We haven't heard from you about what you were able to do so far."

4. **Reflect on the difference between intended and actual outcomes:** "What is getting in the way of your completing (or reporting on) your weekly goals?"

5. **Initiate the choice:** "What will you do going forward and/or what support do you need to be successful?"

ADDRESSING COMMON TEAM PROBLEMS

There are a few problems that seem to come up with most teams: personality conflicts, things getting bogged down, or a team leader who seems to take over rather than lead. Here are some ideas for how to handle these situations:

PERSONALITY CONFLICTS. First, see if the people in conflict are willing to have a direct conversation with each other, at least so they can feel heard and understood by the other person. If that doesn't work, find ways for them not to have to work closely together and remind them that this is a time-limited project and that they're not making a lifelong commitment to each other—all they have to do is get along for this short period of time.

THINGS GET BOGGED DOWN. Figure out one thing you can do to jumpstart the process. For example, if no one is making their follow-up calls, have everyone get out their phones and make one call during the meeting. If the event is getting too complicated, take one element out. One small organization wanted to do a dinner dance with both a silent auction and a live auction. When they realized the plan required too much work and too many logistics, they discussed what would be the most fun and then eliminated both auctions. With much enthusiasm, they then focused on the dinner and dancing. You can always ask the group if they have any ideas for making more progress in the activity. You don't have to have all the answers.

THE TEAM LEADER IS CONTROLLING AND SECOND-GUESSES EVERYONE'S WORK. We often say in fundraising, "If all else fails, try honesty." It also helps to assume good intent, even if a person's behavior leads you to think otherwise. Although many people find it difficult to confront someone who is making life miserable for everyone involved, the alternative is that people stop participating, especially if they are volunteers. It's worth taking the risk to bring up the problem directly and share how their behavior affects you. Be as specific and nonjudgmental as possible. Address this early in the process before you're so angry that you can't have a reasonable conversation.

AFTER THE PROJECT IS COMPLETED: EVALUATION AND APPRECIATION

Often, the aftermath of a major undertaking like this can be a kind of letdown. The team has spent a lot of time making something happen (often more time than they initially expected or thought they had signed on for), and even when the outcome is extremely positive, people can have a feeling of anticlimax. Or, if the event was challenging, people may want to throw in the towel and never show up again to work on your project. Two steps at this phase of the project can help people feel good about what they've done.

The first step is to schedule a final meeting of the entire team to evaluate the project and make any recommendations for future efforts. If the activity was a one-time-only event, this can still be a useful way to give some closure to everyone involved. You can use the Wrap-Up Meeting Agenda as a guide.

SAMPLE WRAP-UP MEETING AGENDA

First, report on the results of the activity:

❑ How much money was raised?

❑ How many people contributed, either by giving money, buying tickets, or in other ways? (This is actually a much more important number than how much money was raised. If one person gave you $2,000 or one hundred people gave gifts of $10 to $250 that totaled $2,000, this tells you a lot more about what happened than just the fact that you raised $2,000.)

❑ How many people volunteered?

❑ Other possible outcomes, such as media coverage (including both traditional media, like your local community paper, and social media) or connections made with people who can be helpful to the project or group in the future.

❑ What new skills did we learn?

❑ Will we do this again in the future?

❑ What else?

Then, to bring in the team's assessment of the project, have them discuss questions like the following:

❑ What do you think went well with this fundraising activity?

❑ What didn't go well?

❑ What did you most enjoy about working on this fundraising activity?

❑ What was most difficult or challenging for you?

❑ How well did you feel the team worked together? What feedback would you give to the people who coordinated or oversaw the process of organizing this activity?

❑ What do you think could be done differently in the future to make the activity more successful, more fun to work on, and able to recruit more people to help out?

❑ Would you participate in an activity like this in the future?

ORGANIZER'S TIPS

As a leader or coleader, you may often find yourself helping to coordinate an activity that you have limited experience doing, or no more experience than the rest of the team. Don't worry! That's how we all learn. Find the balance between being honest with the team that you're learning as well and self-sabotaging by discrediting your ability to take leadership. If you've done the activity once, you can also build up the confidence to train others. For example, if you're coordinating a raffle, sell tickets yourself so you can speak from experience about what works and what doesn't. If you're coordinating a phonebank, take a list and make several calls yourself so you can get comfortable with what you say and test out whether your materials work.

Like you, your team members often are nervous about fundraising or getting the specific strategy right. Being well organized with your materials and conveying some faith and confidence in your team will go a long way toward making them feel confident enough to do the job.

4

The Importance
of "Thank You"

Whatever strategy or combination of strategies you decide to use, thanking people for their support is critical. This includes thanking not only the people who made a monetary contribution but also those who donated their time or made in-kind gifts. (Exceptions might be people who come to your car wash or buy a $5 raffle ticket.) Thanking your supporters is important for a number of reasons:

- People like to feel appreciated. All of us like to know that our contributions are helpful, make a difference, and are acknowledged by those we're supporting.

- A thank-you strengthens your relationship with your supporters and helps them feel good about their relationship with you and the project.

- A thank-you message gives you an opportunity to reinforce your original pitch and add more content, including more about how the funds will be used.

- If there's any chance you'll be going back to your supporters to ask for their help again, whether to renew their donation on an annual basis or for something completely different down the road, you'll have a much better chance of getting someone to give time or money again if you thank them for their gift(s).

- People want to know that their contribution actually arrived. Many donations are now made online or via a payment platform where automated notifications are the norm, so this isn't as critical in most cases as it used to be, but it's important in cases where you received the donation in the mail. And of course, an automated acknowledgment is not the same as a more personalized thank you.

- Because of the number of scandals that have arisen from the nonprofit sector over the years, people also worry that their money has been misused. A follow-up thank-you note, while no real guarantee that the money has been spent properly, gives people some reassurance that it probably has.

The very first thing you do, ideally within a week after a donation is received, is send out a thank-you message. This message could be via email, text, or hard copy note. It could be a phone call or a voice memo. A short recorded video is also a fun way to communicate with your supporters. Get as creative as you'd like with thank yous; what matters most is that you're sharing your gratitude. Here are a few things to remember in crafting thank yous:

- Be sure to thank the donor for exactly what they gave or the volunteer for exactly what they did, such as, "Thank you for your gift of $35," or "Thank you for your donation of one copy of your wonderful book, *Gardening for the Left Handed*," or "Thank you for all the time you put into helping organize the auction. I know we couldn't have done it without you."

- If you as the thanker have a relationship with the person being thanked, acknowledge the importance of your relationship and what it meant for them to volunteer or donate.

- If possible, tell the donor the total you brought in from your fundraising effort: "As you may remember, we needed $5,000 to bring the electrical system in our community center up to code. Thanks to you and one hundred other people, our campaign has already netted $4,500."

If you're raising money for a project or organization that is incorporated as a 501(c)3, or fiscally sponsored by one that is, note the following:

- While it is unlikely you would thank someone who bought an item at an auction or garage sale, if you do acknowledge such a gift, let the donor know that their gift is not tax-deductible. If part of their gift is, in fact, tax-deductible, such as a dinner at a restaurant that normally costs $20 but for which the donor paid $40, let them know that only the amount over the market value of the gift is tax-deductible—in this case, the $20 beyond the value of the meal. Check with your local nonprofit assistance center, volunteer center, or community foundation if you're uncertain about the exact tax deductibility of any gift.

- When nothing of material value has been given to the donor, include this sentence in your thank-you letter: "No goods or services have been exchanged for your gift."

- You are required by law to provide a receipt for any tax-deductible gift of more than $250. A thank-you note specifying the amount given serves as a receipt.

Handwritten (but legible) thank yous can add a personalized touch for the volunteers and donors you're thanking. If you have a manageable number of people to thank, this isn't difficult. You can ask volunteers to help write them.

Here are some sample written thank yous:

Dear Natalia,

Thank you so much for your gift of $35 to help us with the End Prop 13 ballot initiative that is coming up for a vote this November. Your support means a lot to us, and not just financially. Your gift lets us know that there are people in our community who are as excited as we are about this ballot initiative and who are willing to speak out and make a difference. For updates on how this work is going, you can visit endprop13.org.

Thanks again,
(Your name)

Dear Francisco,

When we started our campaign to raise $5,000 to get our bookmobile, people told us there weren't enough people with money in our small town to support this project. Your participation in our bowl-a-thon, for which you brought in $250 in pledges, was a great boost to the campaign. We raised a total of $2,300 from that event, and with the other activities we have planned, we are confident that we'll reach our goal by the end of this year. Thank you for being part of this community effort. The success of this campaign showed us that if people are really committed to something, we are unstoppable!

All the best,
(Your name)

Another way to thank and acknowledge people for their support is to make it public. Here are a few ways to do that:

- If you have a newsletter or other regular way you keep in touch with people, consider including an appreciation page in one issue on which you name everyone who helped out, financially and with their time. Keep in mind that this can be labor intensive because you need to make sure you include everyone who contributed, confirm that they're willing to have their names listed, and spell their names correctly.

- If your community has a local newspaper that covers lots of community events and news, ask the editor to publish a short piece that describes your project, explains how you were able to raise money for it, and mentions the fact that a lot of people came forward to make it a success. If you have photos of an event, a local paper may be willing to include one. This is not as personal for your supporters, but those who were part of the effort will feel proud to see the event in print.

- For an event for which you're handing out a simple program with the order of activities and presentations, you can list the names of any event sponsors who have provided support.

Of all the fundraising-related tasks, sending thank yous has to be the easiest, most rewarding, and most impactful for future volunteering and donating, and yet it is often the most neglected. Make a point to send simple notes to everyone who supports you. People will appreciate it and be more likely to give their time and money again.

5

Building for
the Long Haul

This chapter is focused on laying the groundwork for fundraising efforts that may grow into ongoing projects or organizations. Some of what we address here will also be useful for one-time efforts, though.

Here's an example:

A community that prided itself on a thriving downtown with many independent businesses and few chain stores was approached by a discount big-box store that wanted to open a location a few miles outside of town. With its lower prices (made possible through a badly paid, nonunion workforce) and much-publicized free parking, this store would have likely drawn business from several of the downtown businesses. A small group of community residents got together to fight the opening of the store. With much effort, they enlisted the support of the majority of the town's residents in a campaign to get the city council to deny the store's request. They raised money from community members to pay a community organizer for the year-long campaign. They kept track of everyone who was involved—those who gave money, helped raise money, or helped out in other ways. Several months after winning the big-box-store battle, the community learned that a luxury housing development was being considered that would displace low-income residents. With their list of supporters and volunteers who had worked on the big-box-store campaign, they could quickly gear up to stop the luxury housing development.

After engaging in a successful fundraising activity, you might discover that the need you're raising money for is actually larger and longer term than you initially thought or that you really enjoyed raising money and are ready to commit to continuing the effort.

If you're raising money to organize a one-time conference, rehabilitate an historic building, or send emergency aid to a community that just survived a climate-driven wildfire, you don't need to pay as much attention to infrastructure and record keeping. But even if there's no question in your mind that you're raising money for a one-time need, the experience people have with your project—as volunteers, donors, or supporters—will make them more or less responsive to future activities. So, with the awareness that you never know what needs or opportunities for mobilizing people to action—including donating again—may present themselves down the road, this chapter outlines some things to plan for so that you or others can continue raising money for whatever cause may arise.

RECORD KEEPING

The key to a successful ongoing fundraising program is keeping track of what you do, what the results of your activities are, and who is involved in helping you. Even if you're carrying out a one-time fundraising campaign, creating a simple spreadsheet with information about where your funds came from is a good practice for transparency and communication with your fundraising team. If you want people to give not just one time but once a year or even several times a year over several years, you need to know when and how much they gave and in response to what appeals or circumstances.

If you leave the group, a new person should be able to look at your database, spreadsheet, and/or any paper files you've kept and pick up where you left off.

It's an off-putting experience for your supporters to get a letter or call asking for a contribution that doesn't acknowledge their prior relationship with the organization. This type of oversight is more common than you might think. To help you avoid making that mistake, Worksheet 5.1 provides a simple form for keeping track of everyone who made a donation. If you're tracking donations online, you can use a simple spreadsheet initially. If you decide to do fundraising in a long-term, ongoing way, you'll want to graduate to a more customized fundraising database or constituent relationship management (CRM) software. We recommend starting with an inexpensive, off-the-shelf program, which you can find for $15 per month or less, and then moving on to more powerful—and more expensive—programs as your fundraising program and corresponding budget grow. Researching the best programs can be daunting, but if you're just starting out, it's fine to ask your friends and colleagues who work in nonprofits what they use, and then test a few to get a sense of what might best meet your needs.

WORKSHEET 5.1
Sample Form for Tracking Donors

NAME	EMAIL	PHONE NUMBER	ADDRESS	AMOUNT DONATED	DATE OF DONATION	DATE THANKED	FUNDRAISING STRATEGY	COMMENTS
Jill Chan	chan.jill@gmail.com	123-456-7890	213 Pine St, Tulsa	$50	Aug 12	Sept 3	Phonebank	Former board member
Kyle Davis	kyledavis11@hotmail.com	555-999-6666	555 Oak Dr, Tulsa	$250	Aug 12	Sept 3	Phonebank	Prefers email contact
Josie Sanchez	josie.sanchez@gmail.com	121-232-4343	777 Cedar Ave, Tulsa	$100	Nov 2	Nov 12	House party	Former volunteer, Sam's partner
Craig Yoshikawa	craigy@gmail.com	998-776-5544	954 Birch St, Tulsa	$50	Dec 5	Dec 18	Giving Day peer-to-peer campaign	Don't phone
Sara Nelson	saranelson@gmail.com	312-456-8877	390 Evergreen Lane, Tulsa	$10	Mar 10	Mar 15	Personal ask campaign	Long-time supporter

EVALUATING YOUR FUNDRAISING CAMPAIGN

To learn from what went well and what didn't, document how you accomplished your project. Imagine that a year from now, someone else wants to try organizing a house party, a silent auction, or a phonebank. They can read this book, but an even better teacher will be the actual experience that you had, including how much it cost, who volunteered, who is likely to be willing to volunteer again, how much money you raised, and from how many donors. Record what happened, what took more time than you expected, any changes in the workplan that you would want to implement next time, and anything else that would be useful to someone else who wants to try out this fundraising activity.

RELATIONSHIP BUILDING AND COMMUNITY BUILDING

Fundraising is about much more than getting money to do the things you want to do. It's also about building awareness in the community about community issues and problems, mobilizing people to *do* something (including but not limited to giving money), and giving people a way to take action as part of a larger group in order to have an impact that they couldn't have as individuals acting alone.

Fundraising can help deepen your team's commitment to your group and its mission. By building closer ties to your supporters and everyone who is involved in furthering the mission, you will develop the kinds of personal relationships that will have lasting and continued impact. As fundraising author and trainer Kim Klein says in her article "The Fine Art of Asking for the Gift," (available from Nonprofit Quarterly's archive of the *Grassroots Fundraising Journal*): "Many people have discovered that doing [face-to-face] fundraising reminds them of the true depth of their commitment to an organization. They remember why they became involved with the work in the first place and why they think the work is important."

Ultimately, it's not just the money you raise but the coming together of people who share a vision, a set of beliefs, and the willingness to take action toward a common goal that will lead to success, whatever your cause.

LEADERSHIP DEVELOPMENT

The term *leadership development* has come to encompass everything from community organizing to youth empowerment to skill building in various areas. To some, it means recruiting and training a board of directors, running effective meetings, and managing conflict in a group. In this chapter, leadership development means continually looking for ways to build skills among a group of people in order to develop an ongoing and successful fundraising program that grows and raises more money every year. Even if you're doing a one-off event for a specific purpose, every time you give the people involved more responsibility, you increase the likelihood that they'll take the lead in the next fundraising project. Because even the *idea* of fundraising scares off so many people, it's that much more important to create a plan for involving more people in the work and providing opportunities for people to learn the skills they need to participate effectively.

How do you do this? Here are some suggestions:

- Identify people you think would be well suited for a specific task or committee and invite them personally to get involved. When someone calls Maria and says to her, "I think you'd be a great member of this committee. You have excellent people skills, and because you've lived in this community so long and know all of the merchants on Main Street, you'd probably be able to get more raffle prizes donated than anyone else," you can be sure she'll feel flattered and interested in helping if she can.

- Make the experience of raising money a positive one. Encourage people to do things they are comfortable with initially, then build up to things they feel less sure of.

- Make sure you have enough people, lead time, and upfront funds to implement a given fundraising activity successfully. Don't, for example, plan a major gala with a famous entertainer if you don't have at least six months of lead time, a committee of at least five dedicated people and dozens of others to do specific tasks, the front money (which can be thousands of dollars), and someone who has a real connection to the famous entertainer.

- Find ways for people to learn new skills: bring in a trainer, send people to workshops, role-play, and host practice sessions in the group.

- Don't assume that the best person for any given task is the person who has always done it. Encourage people to try new things and provide supports for them in doing so.

- Before a fundraising activity, do a premortem to help inform your planning: What are potential causes for failure? What are ways we can reduce the risk of failure? What can we do right now as initial steps to reduce that risk?

- Invite feedback after a fundraising activity is completed, with a commitment to incorporate useful ideas the next time. Identify what went well, and don't get defensive if people have a number of ideas about how things could have been better. This is a sign of their ownership and enthusiasm.

- Be scrupulous and transparent about all finances. This is important not only because you want to be responsible about how you raise and use money, but also because people will take on greater responsibility in groups if they understand what it costs to do the work and how the money they're raising is being spent.

NOT BEING A NONPROFIT ORGANIZATION

Many of you who picked up this book are volunteers or staff members of an established (large or small) organization that is incorporated as a nonprofit and has federal tax-exempt status with the tax designation 501(c)3. However, it is perfectly legal to raise money without being part of a nonprofit organization—if you understand a few basic things.

First, you need to decide how you're going to collect and manage the money you raise. You have two choices, each of which has implications for whether your donor can consider their gift tax-deductible:

FIND A NONPROFIT ORGANIZATION IN YOUR COMMUNITY WILLING TO BE YOUR FISCAL SPONSOR. That means they will receive the money, deposit it in their bank account, keep track of it, and then give you the money raised, minus a small fee (usually 6 to 10 percent of what you bring in) to handle their administrative costs. The advantage of this option is that the people making a contribution can get a tax deduction for their gift, and they may feel more assured that their money is being well used. If someone is paying for a car wash or purchasing an item at a garage sale or auction, their payment is *not* a tax-deductible contribution because their payment is in exchange for goods or services received. If they're buying a ticket to your community dinner, you must deduct the fair market value of that dinner from the ticket price when calculating how much of the donation is tax-deductible for the donor. So, for example, if the dinner you're serving would sell for $50 in your community, and the ticket price is $75, the portion of that ticket that is tax-deductible to your donor is $25, not the total cost of $75. (Keep in mind, though, that the vast majority of donors receive no extra tax benefit from their giving because their donations don't exceed the standard deduction. Nevertheless, you are required by law to note the fair market value of goods or services exchanged for a donation if you are doing this work through a tax-exempt entity such as a 501(c)3.)

If you choose to be fiscally sponsored, you need to have a clear understanding of how the financial processes will work, including how your group can review the funding you have on hand, how different forms of payment are processed by your fiscal sponsor (check, online donations, wire/direct deposit), and what processes are required to request and receive funding disbursements.

OPEN YOUR OWN BANK ACCOUNT. If you don't have an organizational bank account and you're raising more than a couple hundred dollars, we encourage you to identify a trusted person to set up a bank account. With a bank account, you can take payment from many online donation platforms, credit cards through a payment processor, and checks.

If you go this route, we recommend keeping records of bank transfers and providing periodic updates to your team about financial transactions. This provides a healthy, transparent team culture in your fundraising and finances. We also recommend setting up an online donation platform that can be connected to your bank account so you can share donation links to potential supporters during your fundraising efforts.

If you decide to open your own bank account rather than find a nonprofit organization to be your fiscal sponsor, *none* of the contributions people make to you will be tax-deductible. For many people, this won't matter, but for larger contributions, donors may be unwilling to make a donation that isn't tax-deductible. Moreover, if you go this route, your donors will need to trust that you are doing what you say you will with the money.

Finally, without the legal structure of a nonprofit organization, you do not have to meet the requirements of providing financial information to anyone who requests it or report your financial activities to the government every year.

PART II

Fundraising
Strategies

The following chapters describe in detail how to implement nine different fundraising strategies. Before deciding on which strategy (or even more than one) you want to carry out, read through each chapter to understand the elements that will make that activity successful, the time required to carry it out, and the ideal number of people needed on your team.

The strategies are divided into three general types of activities. The first category, *direct asks*, involves asking people directly for a contribution. There is no event the donors attend or product they receive in return for their gift. While these are probably the most challenging strategies to implement because they require you to feel comfortable asking for money for your cause, they also tend to generate the most money for the time involved in carrying them out. The second set of strategies, *gatherings*, centers on activities that bring people together—at someone's home, in a larger public setting, or to carry out a pledge-raising event. These are probably the most common fundraising activities the world over and can be a lot of fun. However, because of all the time and effort required to make them successful, they need to be planned carefully and engage a reliable team of volunteers to avoid being a lot of work for little financial return. Finally, *selling* activities generally work because the donor is getting something tangible from the transaction, such as a piece of artwork or a basket of chocolates (auction), a clean car (car wash), a chance at a prize (raffle), or inexpensive secondhand goods (garage sale). For the most part, they are events that most people are familiar with and may have experience doing in other settings. As a result, it's not hard to find a few people to help carry them out, and they can mostly be done without a lot of lead time. Keep in mind that these types of activities don't generally raise as much money as others, especially direct asks for donations.

Each strategy is accompanied by a real-life example of how a group was able to accomplish it with a team composed mostly or entirely of volunteers. We hope these stories will inspire you with their creativity and, in some cases, fun new twists on an old idea.

Every strategy in this book is one that a committed group of volunteers can successfully carry out, and each one comes with its own sets of benefits and challenges. Take the time to consider what your fundraising goals are, which strategy is most likely to work in your community, and which one(s) will bring you the results you're seeking. Don't be tempted to choose a strategy simply because you've heard of it or because you're afraid to take a risk with another strategy—one that might actually benefit your cause more in the long run. The strategy that will work the best is the one that makes the most sense for meeting your goals and that you're able to accomplish with the resources (mostly people!) you have available.

6

Personal Asks

f we were to choose one strategy that is the simplest, most straightforward, and most likely to get you the money you need right *now*, asking someone you know one-on-one would get our vote. And studies of fundraising strategies bear this out. It doesn't require huge amounts of preparation, is less labor-intensive than many other strategies, the costs are minimal, and it can be done very quickly. This strategy involves creating a clear and compelling case for why someone should consider making a gift, coming up with a list of people you know who might be willing to give money to your project, and asking them for a contribution. What the donor receives in return is a heartfelt thank you and the good feeling that they've helped support something or someone they care about.

BEST USES

This strategy is an ideal choice when you need to raise money in a hurry and if the issue you're raising money for is time-specific and compelling to those you're soliciting. For example, people usually respond quickly and with great generosity to disaster-relief efforts because of the urgent and immediate need. Political elections, too, especially highly contested ones, will often generate donations from people who have strong feelings about a candidate or ballot measure. However, asking people one-on-one for financial support can be a successful strategy with any cause or within any time frame as long as you're willing to ask!

Personal asking is a great strategy if you know people you're willing to approach personally and for whom supporting a good cause is important and meaningful. But unlike community fundraisers, raffles, auctions, and other strategies you'll find in this book, you're not offering them anything material (e.g., an experience or an item they might purchase at a garage sale) in return. This strategy can also help deepen relationships with people who give because you're taking the time to speak with them directly, share why you're raising money, and hear what they think about your cause. If you want to fundraise beyond a one-time ask, you can build on these relationships, engage the people who give money, and ask them for another contribution in the future.

THINGS TO CONSIDER

While you can carry out this fundraising strategy by yourself, you'll raise much more money if you can recruit at least a few others to join you in the effort. (Before getting started, make sure to read Chapter 3 on building your fundraising team in addition to the points here.) Plan that each volunteer you recruit will be willing to ask ten to twenty of their friends (and neighbors, family, and so on). With a team of five people, you should be able to raise a few thousand dollars, and possibly a lot more, in just a few weeks.

Finding a team of people to help with personal asks might be a greater challenge than other strategies that involve activities besides asking for money. This is why it's important to build in elements of fun and community building for your volunteers, such as an interactive training to kick off your fundraising efforts or silly prizes for those who solicit the most people or secure the most donations.

COSTS

The costs of doing a one- or two-month individual personal ask drive is minimal: travel to and from the donor, if you're asking in person, and sometimes a meal if you meet with them at a restaurant or café.

MATERIALS NEEDED FOR VOLUNTEERS

Give volunteers copies of Resource B on page 188, Who Can You Ask?, to jog people's minds about their contacts, and Resource C on page 189, Tips on Asking Individuals for Money. In addition, the following materials are described further in the rest of this chapter:

- Sample email, text, voice memo, or voicemail script, and fundraising page if using them, for initial outreach to prospects

- Fact sheet or brief description of the project

- Information on ways to give (QR code and link for online donations, check info, etc.)

- Gift-range chart

STEPS TO TAKE

1. Make a plan and timeline.

2. Recruit volunteers.

3. Make a list of people to ask for donations.

4. Draft sample messages for volunteers to use or adapt; decide whether to use individual fundraising pages (if so, draft a sample fundraising page).

5. Conduct a training and orientation session for volunteers.

6. Start the campaign: everyone sends fundraising appeals to their lists, including a request to meet (phone, virtually, or in person).

7. Meet prospects virtually, in person, or by phone.

8. Track donations, send regular updates, and offer support to volunteers.

9. Send thank yous to donors.

10. Evaluate and thank volunteers.

Step 1: Make a Plan and Timeline

The planning process will help you set a goal for how much money you want to raise, figure out how many volunteers you need to carry out this strategy, and decide if your goals are realistic.

As you start putting your plan together, keep in mind that, generally, more than half of the people you ask directly for a donation will say no, so you need to ask two to three times as many people for a gift as will ultimately give one. Also plan that people will give different amounts of money. Your temptation will be to think, *If I need $5,000 and I can get fifty people to give $100 each, I'll reach my goal.* However, years of fundraising experience have shown that if you ask a cross-section of people to give the same dollar amount (say, $100), you'll lose many contributions from people who would give *something*, but can't afford $100; on the other end of the spectrum, you'll get $100 from people who would be willing and able to give much more. So, if you're trying to raise $5,000, you should plan to get a few contributions of $250 to $500 (and depending on who you're asking, maybe a gift or two of $1,000), a few more between $100 and $250, and lots of contributions of $50 or less. Putting these numbers together into a planning tool called a *gift-range chart* will help you figure out how many contributions of what amounts you'll need to reach your goal.

It's also important to give your potential donors a clear idea of what you want from them. Just saying, "Give and be as generous as you can" is too vague and leaves people with the uneasy feeling that they don't know how much is generous enough or even how much you need. Data shows that people won't buy a product in a store if the price isn't clear.

Another advantage of preparing a gift-range chart is that it's something you can share with prospective supporters, which can be reassuring to them because it shows that you've thought through what you need to be successful.

To create a gift-range chart, start with your fundraising goal (for example, $5,000). The largest gift you'll be seeking is one that equals 10 percent of the goal (in this example, $500). Why start there? Over decades of experience with fundraising campaigns, we've observed that donations tend to come in like this: very few at the highest level of your chart, more at the mid-level, and most gifts at smaller amounts. Even if gifts come in at amounts that don't exactly match the gift-range chart, in your planning, you'll want to aim to get two gifts at that top level, or 20 percent of your goal, from the amount raised at this level. The total amount you want to raise at the next-largest gift level should also equal 20 percent. You'll need more gifts at that level to reach that goal. Continue constructing your chart, as shown in Worksheet 6.1, so that the number of gifts you expect to receive at each level *increases* as the dollar amount of each level *decreases*.

Don't get too bogged down in making your gift-range chart. There is no completely scientific way to do it. What matters is that you have an initial plan to help drive your fundraising efforts.

The sample gift-range chart in Worksheet 6.1 shows a typical distribution of gifts you're likely to receive at different levels, and gives you an idea of how many people you need to ask to reach your goal. In this chart, you can see that you would need about 70 contributions of varying amounts to reach your goal of $5,000. That means you need about 140 people to ask to ensure you'll reach your goal.

WORKSHEET 6.1
Gift Range Chart

NUMBER OF GIFTS	AMOUNT	NUMBER OF PEOPLE TO ASK	TOTAL
2	$500	6	$1,000
4	$250	8–12	$1,000
12	$100	24	$1,200
20	$50	40	$1,000
32	$25	64	$800
TOTAL			
70	—	·140	$5,000

Your group could also consider doing a fundraising campaign as part of a Giving Day, which is a designated fundraising day organized by a nonprofit, often a community foundation, to promote donations to nonprofits. As of this writing, the largest and most well-known one is Giving Tuesday, which takes place the Tuesday after Thanksgiving. There are also Giving Months; for example, #GiveInMay, in honor of Asian American and Pacific Islander Heritage Month, is sponsored by the Asian Pacific Fund and other community partners. Giving Days can be helpful for people hesitant about fundraising because it's a dedicated day where making asks is normalized and common.

One challenge with Giving Tuesday is that it comes at a time of year when donation requests are at their peak for many nonprofits and causes. This means you risk getting drowned out in the noise of all the other appeals your potential donors are getting. However, over the years, we've been surprised to discover that groups sometimes have more success with Giving Tuesday–type events than when they try to implement campaigns of personal asking that lack that kind of "buzz."

Other Giving Days, such as Arizona Gives, avoid the competition of Giving Tuesday and other year-end fundraising campaigns. However, there is still the issue of competition for the attention and support of people who may be getting requests from several groups participating in a particular Giving Day.

Step 2: Recruit Volunteers

Personal asks are one of the few strategies in this book that you *can* do by yourself, but they won't be as much fun and you won't raise as much money as you will if more people are involved. Use Resource A, the Volunteer Recruitment Form, to help you come up with the names of potential volunteers. Here are the tasks you'll be recruiting people to do:

- Come up with names of people to ask for donations.

- Draft a sample email or text message asking people to meet—by phone, in person, or virtually.

- If using fundraising pages, draft a sample page.

- Make the ask!

Not everyone on the team has to do everything. You need to have at least a few people willing to ask their friends for money, but if someone really doesn't want to do that, they can help write the sample messages or keep track of information on donors and their contact information for any next steps.

If you have a large fundraising goal and would like to recruit a lot of askers, you can recruit team captains, who are tasked with building a team of three to six people from their network, who in turn will ask other people in their network to donate. Under this model, team captains work with the core organizers to give and receive updates, troubleshoot, and adapt based on the campaign's goals.

Step 3: Make a List of People to Ask for Donations

After finding volunteers to help you carry out this fundraising activity, the key to success is coming up with a list of people to ask for money. Your first task as a committee, then, is for each member to come up with as many names as possible. A good time for this to occur is during the initial meeting and training of volunteers (see Step 5). Use Resource B, on page 188, Who Can You Ask?, for ideas on whom to put on your list. Each volunteer can put their name on their copy of Worksheet 6.2. See sample on following page.

Once you've brainstormed the names of everyone you know, have each volunteer use Worksheet 6.2 to identify the following information about each person:

- What is your relationship with them (and how strong is the relationship)?

- Are they likely to believe in this project (or at least not be opposed to it)?

- Are they donors to your group already or to similar groups or causes?

Ideally, all of these names are stored in the same spreadsheet, database, or folder that you can reference throughout your fundraising efforts.

Use this form to create your list of people to ask for a donation. Refer to Resource B on page 188, Who Can You Ask?, to develop ideas that may not have occurred to you. Once you've created your list, decide how much money you'll request from each person. If you have absolutely no idea, then suggest a range, such as $25 to $100, or $250 to $500. While many people are uncomfortable asking for a specific amount, from the prospective donor's point of view, it helps give them an idea of what you need and how they can help. And, of course, you can always add that a gift of any size is greatly appreciated.

The people most likely to give money from the lists compiled are those who care about the cause and who give money away, as evidenced by being members of or donors to other groups or belonging to a house of worship. Start with them.

WORSHEET 6.2
Potential Supporters

NAME	EMAIL	PHONE NUMBER	ADDRESS	RELATIONSHIP TO YOU	CARES ABOUT CAUSE?	GIVES AWAY MONEY?	HOW MUCH TO ASK FOR	COMMENTS
Yolanda Johnson	yolanda.johnson@gmail.com	123-456-7890	213 Pine St, Tulsa	Sister	Yes	Yes	$100	
Brian Park	park.brian @gmail.com	555-999-6666	555 Oak Dr, Tulsa	Neighbor	Not sure	Not sure, but he's a member of local church	$15–25	
Jessica Liu	jessical22 @gmail.com	121-232-4343	777 Cedar Ave, Tulsa	Previous supporter of the group	Yes	Yes	$500	

Step 4: Draft Sample Messages and Fundraising Pages as Needed

Providing the team with sample messages will speed up the process of getting them to schedule their asks. Encourage people to adapt the examples to their own voices and reasons for being involved in the effort. Share with them the Tips on Writing an Email Appeal and sample letters that follow.

TIPS ON WRITING AN EMAIL APPEAL

In simple, straightforward language, tell the person what you're raising money for. Telling a story about someone affected by the issue gets the reader's attention better than broad, sweeping statements. (See the sample letter about the wildfire in Maui.)

Tell them what your relationship to the issue is. The person you're asking has a relationship with you, so it helps them to see why you feel connected to the issue.

Be specific about what you want. Telling your potential supporters how much money you need to raise and the size of contributions you're looking for gives them a way to think about an appropriate amount to donate.

State in the initial communication that you would like to schedule a time to discuss the request with them. This is especially important if you're asking for a large gift (e.g., $500 or more). This shows that you know it's something they have to give some thought to, and it also provides them with an opportunity to ask questions or just discuss the request with you.

Here are some sample letters:

TO CONTINUE A SCHOOL MUSIC PROGRAM

Dear Maria,

I think you know how much our kids love the music classes they've taken in school, including the opportunity to perform with the choir every year. What you may not know is that as a result of the recent state cuts in education funding, all music instruction will be eliminated starting in the fall. Many of the parents are getting together to see what we can do to get the funding reinstated. In the meantime, we're trying to raise $20,000 to keep at least one part-time music teacher on staff for the next school year.

I'm writing to you as someone who believes that education is about more than just "the basics," that it includes subjects like music and art. While we fight to get the funding back, we're hoping that friends like you will consider making a contribution toward our goal of $20,000. Any amount will help—$10, $25, $100, or even more—but before you decide, I'd like to talk with you briefly.

I'm available next week, either for a phone call or in person at our favorite café, on Wednesday morning 9:30 to noon or Thursday all day. Which of those works best for you?

I really appreciate you considering this request.

Sincerely,

TO SUPPORT DISASTER RELIEF EFFORTS

Dear Cole,

As you know, the recent fire in Maui left our community totally devastated. In addition to the loss of many lives, the fire caused thousands of people to lose their homes. I am so thankful that my grandparents and cousins who still live there are all safe, but as with so many, their homes suffered a lot of damage. Until repairs are made, they are staying with friends who live in a town nearby.

I'm writing to ask for your help. I've joined with a group of people who live on the mainland and have family in Maui to raise $50,000 to help repair homes there. Even though the total costs are much higher because of the challenges folks are facing with getting needed support from FEMA, these funds will truly make a difference.

I hope you can make a donation. We're looking for contributions of $25 to $1,000. Of course, any amount is greatly appreciated. I'll call you soon to talk to you about this request and answer any questions you may have. In the meantime, you can also make a donation anytime at this secure site [include link to the donation page].

I'm available next week, either for a phone call or in person at our favorite café, on Wednesday morning 9:30 to noon or Thursday all day. Which of those works best for you?

Thank you so much for considering this request.

A GIVING TUESDAY APPEAL

Dear Latonya,

I hope this letter finds you well.

As you know, last year the LGBTQ Community Center opened in a large room in the basement of the Quaker Meeting House here in our small town. Since it opened, more than twenty events have been held there, with more than one thousand people attending in all. Some people have driven more than four hours from their ranches and farms to attend. Our hotline receives ten or more calls a day, and we have recently opened a small LGBTQ library and "coffee shop" (basically a couch and chair near the sink, with a coffee pot). It is simple, but it's so important that LGBTQ people have a local place to call our own.

This year, we need to raise $10,000 to cover the costs of rent and a part-time organizer, and we've decided to participate in Giving Tuesday (which is today!). My personal goal is to raise $500 toward the goal. I am hoping you will help with a gift of between $50 and $100, but any amount is greatly appreciated.

Here's a link [include link to donation page] to our Giving Tuesday page with more information about our work and about how to make a donation.

Thank you in advance for helping out with this!

Sincerely,

Consider whether you would like participants to have their own individual fundraising pages, like Haley's in the example on the following page. Many online fundraising platforms offer this feature free of charge.

When participants create their own fundraising pages, they can track who's given and at what amount so they can follow up with people in their networks—to thank them if they have given or check in with them if they haven't. It also allows participants to customize the page to add why they're fundraising for your cause. On the other hand, it's an additional step for participants, which could create a drawback for participation, particularly for those who are less tech-comfortable.

Deadlift & Drag

♦ DEADLIFT MEET
AUGUST 13 2022
10AM – 1PM
♦ LIVE DJ DRAG SHOW
AFTER PARTY AT ALOHA CLUB
2PM – 4PM
BENEFIT FOR TGIJP & RADICALLY FIT
QTBIPOC CENTERED ♦ OPEN TO ALL ♦ NOTAFLOF

Organized by Radically Fit →

$6,855   155 Supporters

Haley Bash
Fundraiser since Jun 2022

↥ Share Haley Bash's Page

$2,056 63 supporters   82% of $2,500 goal

Haley Bash's Story

I'm taking my day-to-day work of donor organizing to something that's a bit more personal: I'm queer. I'm nonbinary. And what gives me the most joy is lifting heavy things. This will be my first ~public debut~ outside of my garage gym. This is bringing my two greatest loves - deadlift and drag - together. But even more important than that, proceeds go to two orgs I care about deeply: Transgender, Gender Variant & Intersex Justice Project (TGIJP) & Radically Fit. Who doesn't love deadlifting, drag, AND supporting trans+queer liberation? My 30th birthday is right around lift date. The best present for my peak Leo energy is a donation that's meaningful to you to orgs that are fighting for the change we want to see in the world. Loveyoumeanit!

If you don't go with individual fundraising pages, make a plan for how your team members can track which people on their respective lists have given. Some groups do this by giving each fundraiser a unique referral code, or refcode (a code that the fundraiser includes in the URL they send with their email or text message to their list of prospective donors). For example, if the volunteer's name is Manu, the refcode could be "manu," and all donations made from clicking on their link will be tracked as having come from Manu). Other groups have a weekly or daily check-in to review the full list of donors and have participants indicate which donations came from people on their list.

If you decide to use individual fundraising pages, draft a sample page so people can see how to answer the following questions:

- Why does this matter?
- Why do we need to act now?
- How will the funds be used?
- Why should your friends/family/other contacts be a part of it?
- How much are you raising?
- By when do you need it?

Step 5: Conduct a Training and Orientation Session for Volunteers

Because this strategy of asking individuals to give money is not done in a group, but one person at a time, volunteers can feel somewhat disconnected from the larger effort. It is therefore important to bring everyone together at the beginning of the campaign to get clear instructions and some training on how to ask for money and to build the excitement of a team working together toward a common goal.

At this session, which should take 1.5 to 2.5 hours, volunteers will have a chance to talk about any anxieties they have about asking for money, learn skills to make them more comfortable asking, learn more about the project or cause for which they're raising money, and complete their lists of people to ask. Use the Sample Agenda for the Orientation and Training Session to guide you.

SAMPLE AGENDA
for the Orientation and Training Session

1. Welcome and introductions. People share why they've agreed to participate in this fundraising project.

2. Discuss the goals and process of the campaign: how much money you want to raise, what the money is for, how long the campaign will last, and approximately how many people will need to be asked for money.

3. Answer any questions people have about the fundraising effort itself.

4. Have a discussion about people's fears and anxieties about asking for money. Give volunteers a chance to talk about their feelings. Emphasize that most people find asking for money challenging at first but, with a little practice, it's not as scary as they thought.

5. Do a brief presentation on the process of asking: people will reach out to a contact, schedule a one-on-one conversation, and ask for the contribution on a phone call, video call, or in person.

6. Role-play so that people can practice making a phone call to ask someone for money.

7. Put together lists of people to ask.

8. If there's time, have people start reaching out to their list.

Step 6: Start the Campaign

Immediately after the training and orientation session, volunteers should complete and send their requests. Some groups find it easier to add another hour to the training and have everyone begin reaching out to their contacts.

This outreach should include specific dates and times the volunteer is available to speak with the potential donor. Personal notes are an important touch because the relationship with potential donors is one of the main reasons they donate.

You can expect that about 10 to 20 percent of the people who receive your request will send in a donation without a scheduled meeting. You can easily double that response by meeting, and sometimes just offering to meet will increase the response.

Step 7: Meet Prospects Virtually, in Person, or by Phone

This step is the most difficult task for many people who are reluctant to solicit someone directly for a contribution. However, if your volunteers don't make these asks, far fewer people will send in a contribution. And remember that people appreciate the personal connection.

It's helpful to remind volunteers that since they're reaching out to their own personal networks, they should make the purpose of the call clear at the beginning of the conversation. Certainly, it's important and natural to chat and catch up with friends or family, but it may feel awkward to bring up the fundraising ask after talking for a while. It's also helpful to state the purpose of the call up front to give the conversation a clear focus and not stray too far from the goal of sharing the project and asking them to help.

If the volunteer's list includes people they think could give $500 or more, the volunteer should offer to meet with them in person unless they live far away. In-person meetings are much more effective because people expect to spend more time in a face-to-face meeting than on a phone call (though you don't generally need more than thirty minutes for the meeting), and when someone is willing to take the time to meet with you, they're very likely to say yes to your request for support. See Tips on Making Phone Calls for Personal Asks for some guidelines.

TIPS ON MAKING PHONE CALLS FOR PERSONAL ASKS

❏ Relax and be yourself—you're calling people who know and like you!

❏ Remind the person why you're calling near the beginning of the conversation.

❏ Assume support, be confident, and be as direct as possible ("We're working to win . . . " or "I know this issue is something you and I both care a lot about").

❏ Use your own words. Don't read from a script.

❏ Listen; give people a chance to speak, ask a question, or voice an opinion about the issue. Don't talk *at* them; instead, aim for an interaction. You may be surprised that your prospect is already interested in what you're raising money for or wants to share their thoughts and concerns.

❏ If someone asks you a question that you don't know the answer to, be honest and tell them you don't know. Let them know you'll get back to them (and then make a note of it and *do* get back to them or make sure someone else does).

❏ Keep it short and simple. Be clear, concise, and direct.

❏ Ask for a specific amount of money.

❏ Once you make the ask, be silent. Let them think about it and answer. If you need to, slowly count to twenty in your head to keep yourself from filling the space with nervous chatter.

❏ Once they make a specific commitment, thank them and make sure they have what they need to make a contribution. If they need to think about it, ask if there are any questions you can answer right now. If they still need to think, make a specific time to call them back (and then follow up).

❏ Thank them for their time.

❏ Remember that practice makes perfect!

See the Sample Script for Follow-Up Virtually, in Person, or by Phone on the following page for an example of making an ask on a scheduled call. You can adapt the basic structure outlined here depending on the issue you're raising money for and who you're talking to. Your volunteers can use this as a guideline, but emphasize that they shouldn't read from a script; they should use their own words.

SAMPLE SCRIPT
for Follow-Up Virtually, in Person, or by Phone

STRUCTURE OF THE CALL	WHAT TO SAY
Introduction: who you are, brief greeting, purpose of call.	Hi [their name], this is Kai. Is now still a good time to chat? (If they say no, reschedule.) How are you? [Quick small talk here.] As I mentioned in my text, I've been active with the Maui Relief Effort.
Explain problem and what you're raising money for: speak briefly about the project you're raising money for.	The text I sent you a few days ago is about the recent wildfire in Maui and the work some of us are doing to raise money to help with relief efforts. As you know, the fire last month caused not only millions of dollars' worth of damage, but also left a lot of people homeless. My grandparents' home was destroyed. I'm grateful that my grandparents and cousins who live there are safe, but they'll need at least $10,000 to rebuild, and FEMA will only cover a small portion of that. I'm calling everyone I know to ask if they can donate some money for this cause.
Ask if they have questions.	Do you have any questions? (Pause and wait for them to respond. Once you've answered their questions, continue.)
Ask for a contribution.	Your support would be such an incredible help to the residents of Maui. Do you think you could give $50? (At this point, stop and listen.)
If they say yes . . .	Thanks so much! How would you like to donate? (Give them information based on what they share—a link to donate online, check information, etc.)
If they say no . . .	Thank you for taking the time to talk to me. Can I come back to you another time? (If they say they just can't afford to give right now, and you will be doing another fundraising campaign in the future, it's a good idea to ask if you can contact them again. If they really aren't interested in your project, just thank them and say goodbye.)
If they hesitate or seem unsure . . .	(Ask if they have more questions or if they need time to think about it.)
Thank them!	Thank you for taking the time to talk to me. I really appreciate it.

Use Worksheet 6.3 to keep track of your requests for support. It's easy to forget who you called, when you left a message, and how much they said they'd give if you don't keep your data up to date.

WORKSHEET 6.3
Sample Tracking Form for Asks Made

PROSPECT NAME	DATE REACHED OUT	DATE MEETING TOOK PLACE OR CONTACT MADE	RESULTS/NOTES	AMOUNT PLEDGED	DATE RECEIVED	AMOUNT RECEIVED	DATE THANK YOU SENT
Yolanda Johnson	10/12	10/20	Agreed to donate; didn't want to meet	$50	10/21	$50	10/28
Brian Park	10/12	10/25	No, but maybe another time				
Sue Stein	10/15	11/1	Met for coffee and ask	$250	11/5	$250	11/6

If volunteers have extra enthusiasm after making their asks to ten to twenty people, encourage them to make lower-effort asks to people who are likely supportive of the cause but weren't part of their initial ten-to-twenty-person list. These can be direct fundraising asks through email, text, and voice memos, as well as indirect fundraising asks through social media.

You'll likely get smaller gifts from email, text, and voice memo asks than you would for a one-on-one ask that you do by phone, in person, or virtually. And you'll also get fewer gifts as a percentage of the people you ask than with a one-on-one request. Plan on about 10 to 25 percent of the people you know and solicit by email, text, and voice memo donating to your fundraising campaign.

Step 8: Track Donations, Send Regular Updates, and Offer Support to Volunteers

While volunteers are making their asks, the core organizers (and team captains, if you have them) are tasked with tracking donations and communicating updates to volunteers and donors. This is generally done on a weekly basis unless the campaign is running on a very short timeline and you need more frequent updates. The goals in this step are for

- volunteers to share updates on their asks, pledges, and donations and share any ideas and challenges they're facing; and

- the core organizers or team captains to provide volunteers with soundboarding, troubleshooting, and updates on the total raised so far that they can share with donors in their network.

Step 9: Send Thank Yous to Donors

As soon as possible after you receive someone's contribution, send them a thank you. If you get your volunteers together for an evaluation, you could bring blank thank-you notes for people to write together.

Step 10: Evaluate and Thank Volunteers

When you finish the project, come back together with your volunteers to evaluate your efforts. How much money did you raise collectively? How many people were asked, and how many gave? Celebrate and recognize people's efforts. What worked? What would you do differently next time? Even if you did not meet your goals, what were lessons learned? You want people to have a good experience and to learn from this effort so that they will continue working on the project and increase their enthusiasm for fundraising.

Jewish Youth for Community Action

Jewish Youth for Community Action was an organization based in Oakland, California, that developed the leadership skills of high-school-age Jewish youth as they became involved in social action and community projects. Because there were very few paid staff, fundraising activities were carried out by the youth and their parents. Once a year, they sent out hard-copy fundraising letters (this was before email was widespread) to their friends, family members, alumni of the program, and past donors to the project. The fundraising team then made follow-up calls to everyone who received a letter. After several years of these annual appeals, they were able to count on raising a good percentage of their budget from this very grassroots, but direct asking, effort.

WORKPLAN

Workplan 6.1 (on the following page) summarizes the key steps necessary to implement this fundraising strategy and an estimated time frame for each step. It is meant to be a template from which to create your own plan and your own timeline. By taking the time to create a plan and timeline, you'll be more organized, more likely to avoid last-minute crises, and ultimately more successful in raising the money you need.

WORKPLAN 6.1
The Personal Ask

WHAT	WHO	1	2	3	4	5	6	7	8	DONE
1. Make a plan and timeline.		×								
Create a gift-range chart.		×								
2. Recruit volunteers.		×								
3. Make a list of people to ask for donations.		×	×							
4. Draft sample messages for volunteers to use or adapt; decide whether to use individual fundraising pages (if so, draft a sample fundraising page).			×							
5. Conduct a training and orientation session for volunteers.				×						
6. Start the campaign: everyone sends fundraising appeals to their lists, including a request to meet (virtually, in person, or by phone).				×						
7. Meet prospects virtually, in person, or by phone.					×	×	×	×		
8. Track donations, send regular updates, and offer support to volunteers.					×	×	×	×	×	
9. Send thank yous to donors.								×	×	
10. Evaluate the effort and thank volunteers.									×	

The "WHEN (WEEK NUMBER)" columns span week numbers 1–8.

7

Phonebanks

Phonebanking for fundraising involves making calls to a list of people who have been identified as likely to respond positively to a request for support. Phonebanks involve a group of people coming together at one time (in person or virtually) to call a large number of people for a specific reason—in this case, to raise money. What differentiates a phonebank from a personal ask campaign is that a phonebank takes place at a specific time or on a few different days or evenings; involves calling as many people as possible, many of whom the phonebankers won't personally know; and the calls themselves generally last only a few minutes (for the few people you actually get to talk to). The fundamental requirements of a phonebank are 1) at least four or five people making calls, and 2) a sufficient number of people to call. Generally, one person can call thirty or more people in an hour because for most calls, they'll have to leave a message, meaning each call is quite short.

Phonebanking is a great way to reach a lot of people very quickly. The more people you have calling, the more people you'll reach. If you have a list of five hundred people to call, for example, it is far faster (and more fun) to do it with ten people during an evening than for one person to spend seventeen hours making calls by themselves. Another advantage to a well-run phonebank is that it's a great way to deepen your relationships with the people making the calls. When people get together to carry out a shared task, they're likely to feel more connected to the group. Phonebanks can be fun if you create a supportive and enjoyable atmosphere. Cheer people on, feed them, and share with each other why this cause is important to all of you.

A challenge to overcome with phonebanks is that many people won't answer their phone if they don't know the identity of the person calling, so plan that you'll probably reach just a handful of people over the course of an evening. However, if your list is made up of at least some people who are known to your callers, you'll get more people answering their calls. And those who do pick up the phone tend to respond more positively if they know that the phonebanker is a volunteer, as a person taking their time to make phone calls for your project generally believes strongly in what the project is doing. That connection and commitment come through over the phone and are often contagious.

Phonebanks can be stand-alone fundraising activities or used to follow up an email asking for money. When combined with an email, the phonebank can be an effective way to have more personal contact, interact and answer questions, and ask for a donation. Sending out a mass email ahead of time letting people know you'll be calling them on a certain date can help increase the chances that people will answer the phone. It can also lessen volunteers' anxiety about making calls when they can say, "I'm calling to follow up on the email I sent you last week about this important issue I'm raising money for. Did you have a chance to read it?"

BEST USES

Phonebanks work best when you have a lot of people you want to ask and not enough time to approach each one more personally. Because of the negative associations with phone solicitations, this strategy also works best when the people you're calling know you or when you have some idea that they'll be receptive to the cause for which you're raising money.

THINGS TO CONSIDER

If you don't have at least two hundred names to call, you should probably try a different strategy. The volume of calls is what makes phonebanks successful. You also need to find volunteers who are not intimidated by asking for money by phone and who can be cheerful and friendly on the phone.

The National Do Not Call Registry does *not* apply to nonprofits and charitable organizations. Since October 1, 2003, consumers have been able to register their phone numbers with this federal registry, which prevents businesses from calling to solicit them. Organizations exempt from this law include charities or nonprofit organizations, organizations engaged in political solicitations or surveys, and sellers or telemarketers that call *only* consumers with whom they have an established business relationship or have obtained express written agreement to call. You may want to share this information with your volunteers to reassure them that you can legally call your list. You may, however, still come across an irate person or two who does not want to be called whether they are in the Do Not Call Registry or not. Take those people off your list and tell them you are doing so. However, you should confirm whether the person still wants to remain on the group's email list.

Generally, most phonebankers use their own cell phones to make calls. If phonebankers prefer not to have their phone numbers visible to the folks they're calling, they can get a new phone number using a free or low-cost service available for this purpose, which enables the caller to make calls and access voicemail. The new phone number generated can be in the area code in which your group is based, which makes it more likely that the calls will be picked up.

For very large lists, consider investing in phonebanking software to reduce manual time spent on dialing phone numbers. Phonebanking software generally charges per minute or per call for pay-as-you-go plans. For groups that plan on phonebanking regularly, many platforms offer monthly subscription fees.

COSTS

You can expect to incur the following costs when doing a phonebank:

- Refreshments for volunteers (can be donated)
- Materials for volunteers:
    - Tally sheets
    - Script
    - Fact sheet (how to answer common questions)
    - Call list and tracking form
    - Items to make the phonebank fun, such as prizes or noisemakers for people to set off when they get a pledge
    - Printed pledge forms and details about what you're raising money for to send to people who ask for more information to be mailed to them (optional)
    - Phonebanking software (optional; recommended only for very large lists)

STEPS TO TAKE

1. Make a plan.

2. Recruit volunteers.

3. Get/create lists of people to call.

4. Find a location for the phonebank.

5. Prepare materials.

6. Make final preparations.

7. Train volunteers and carry out the phonebank.

8. Wrap up and send thank yous.

As you go through the steps in detail, use the sample workplan at the end of the chapter to create a timeline and task list.

Step 1: Make a Plan

Decide how much money you want to raise, then figure out how many people you need to call to reach that goal. Here's how to make those calculations:

- One phonebanker will average about thirty calls per hour.

- Approximately six people will answer the phone (and sometimes fewer).

- One or two of those people are likely to say yes to making a donation.

- Donations will average $35, though you will often receive gifts of $15 or $20 and a few at $100 or more.

Using these rates, you can calculate how many people you need to call. If, for example, your goal is to raise $2,500, and you expect an average gift of $35, you would need seventy-one gifts to reach your goal, and to call fifteen hundred to three thousand people. With each phonebanker getting through a list of sixty names in one evening, you need between twenty and forty people calling. Another option is to have a smaller group of phonebankers making calls over several nights. Aim to have at least five people, which is a number that creates a mood of excitement and a feeling of "We're in this together."

Step 2: Recruit Volunteers

Using the Volunteer Recruitment Form in Resource A, identify people who might be willing to help. If you're part of an established organization, you'll want to ask staff members, board members, volunteers, members, donors, and anyone else who has a positive relationship with the group. While your priority is to find people who are willing to come to the phonebank and make calls, here are some other tasks volunteers can do:

- Find a place to hold the phonebank.

- Help come up with lists of people to call.

- Create the script.

- Help with logistics and arrangements for the day of the phonebank.

Start recruiting people to make calls six to eight weeks before the phonebank. Make reminder calls and texts the week before the phonebank and again one or two days in advance. Don't just rely on email for reminders: one-on-one outreach by text or phone leads to greater likelihood of follow-through from RSVP to attendance.

Usually, about half of the people who initially say they'll participate in the phonebank will actually show up. If you need five volunteers to make your phonebank successful, recruit eight to ten volunteers, depending on how committed your volunteers are.

Step 3: Get/Create Lists of People to Call

Think about who you are calling and why. The size and quality of the lists of names you call are probably the two most important factors in how well your phonebank will do. You can have the best phonebankers, the most delicious food, the nicest office space, and the most compelling reason to be calling, but if you're calling people who don't support your cause, or don't know anything at all about your project, or if you just don't have enough people to call, you will have a difficult time raising the money you need.

A high-quality list contains more than just names and phone numbers. It's best if you have some information about the people you're calling, either from their member or donor records if they are past supporters of the group or from information you gather from the people who gave you the names. The information can be as basic as who knows them or if and when they've given money before and how much, or as detailed as how they got involved with your group. Any information you can pass on to the phonebankers will be helpful for their calls. Part of the benefit of a phonebank is to be able to update the information you have about the people in your database. New or wrong numbers are important to note, along with any relevant information you might learn during a call. It's also important to be able to write notes from the call right on the list, such as "No answer," "Left message," or "Call back Tuesday." These notes will inform the next person who calls whether or not you had some contact with the person.

A phonebank differs from other strategies in this book in that you need to have larger lists of people to ask. If each phonebanker can get through a list of sixty names in one evening and you're aiming to recruit at least five phonebankers, you'll need at least three hundred names to call in order to create the energy, momentum, and ultimate success in meeting your goals.

If your group already has a list of people they know and have had even limited contact with, that's a good place to start. Sign-in sheets from events you've had are a great source, for example. If you don't have sign-in sheets, consider making them a regular part of all your events so you can build your list of contacts for future fundraising. You can also use the worksheet in Resource B on page 188, Who Can You Ask?, to gather names and phone numbers of people your phonebank volunteers know.

Step 4: Find a Location for the Phonebank

Once you've identified who is making the calls and who you're calling, you need a place to make the calls. Phonebanks can be done in person with attendees at the same physical location or virtually with attendees present at the same time. Everyone making calls at the same time makes training and troubleshooting efforts easier and less time-consuming and builds camaraderie and momentum as the team works through call lists together.

Virtual phonebanks are ideal if convening in person is logistically difficult for participants (they're geographically far apart, have schedules that make commute times a barrier, etc.) or if finding a physical location feels onerous.

If your phonebank is in person, the following questions should help lead you to the location you need:

- *Do you or any other volunteers work in an office?* Most phonebanks take place outside of regular work hours, from 5:00 or 6:00 P.M. to 8:00 P.M. on weeknights or on Sunday afternoons, when most people are not in the office. Keep in mind, too, that you may be calling people in different time zones, so plan around that when scheduling the phonebank.

- *Is your location in a building with other groups that would let you use their office?* Just make sure you ask one or two weeks ahead (or however much time you think they will need) and make all the arrangements clear: how to get into the office and lock up, where the restrooms are, and so on. It's easier to coordinate a phonebank if all the phonebankers are in the same office, but it's possible to coordinate phonebanks in different offices that are close to each other.

- *Can you find an organization in your community (not necessarily in your building)?* If you have a relationship with a local business, a union, or another organization, look into borrowing their offices for an evening phonebank and make the same arrangements just described.

Step 5: Prepare Materials

Each phonebanker should have access to the following items:

- Tally sheet
- Summary tally sheet
- Call script
- Call list
- Pledge forms

Tally Sheets

Prepare two kinds of tally sheets: one for each person making calls and one that tabulates the totals of all the calls made during the phonebank. For virtual phonebanks, these should be in spreadsheet format so everyone is working from the same data. In-person phonebanks can use spreadsheet or paper tally sheets. If using spreadsheets in person, you'll want to make sure all phonebankers have access to them through their phone or laptop.

An individual's tally sheet, as in Worksheet 7.1 on the following page, should include the phonebanker's name, the date, and the total amount of time they spent calling. It's also good to have spaces to record how many calls were made, how many people were actually reached, how many said yes or no, and the amount of money raised.

The summary tally sheet will include the totals from all of the individual tally sheets. The summary tally is important because it lets you monitor how your phonebank is really doing. At the end of the day, if your results are significantly less than what you expected, try to figure out what's working and what's not. This information will be informed by feedback from your phonebankers at the end of the day's calls. Worksheet 7.2 provides a sample summary tally sheet.

WORKSHEET 7.1
Phonebank: Sample Individual Tally Sheet

Volunteer name	Carly Washington
Date	2/11/2025
Number of hours calling (in 15-minute increments)	2 hrs, 15 mins
Attempts	65
Contacts	7
Pledges made	3
Donations made	2
Total amount raised	$175
Nos	4
"Take me off your list"	2

WORKSHEET 7.2
Sample Consolidated Tracking Sheet

VOLUNTEER NAME	HOURS	ATTEMPTS	CONTACTS	DONATIONS	TOTAL PLEDGES	TOTAL RAISED	NOS
Maria	4	96	12	3	$200	$200	8
John	3	80	8	2	$100	$50	5
May	4	83	8	2	$120	$80	6
Carly	2.25	55	6	1	$70	$70	5
Hal	2.5	60	10	1	$200	$100	5

Call Script

The best call script is a simple one. Think of the script as an outline of where you want the conversation to go. Most importantly, people should try not to read the script to the listener, but to engage them in a brief conversation. Having said that, let your phonebankers know that it's okay to read catchphrases or succinct points from the script, but if they start to read whole chunks of the script, the person on the other end will tune them out.

The goal is to sound as genuine as possible. Phonebankers should talk to the person on the other end as if they're talking to a friend. That doesn't mean being too casual. Phonebankers can still sound professional without being too formal. The Call Script Outline will give you a basic structure.

CALL SCRIPT OUTLINE

Introductions

❏ Introduce yourself and the group you're calling about.

❏ Tell them why you're calling ("I'm calling to talk to you about the Campaign for Better Bike Lanes and to ask for your support.")

Engaging the Prospect

❏ Ask them if they've heard of the group or campaign, and if they have, ask what they think about it, or what their involvement has been.

❏ Before moving on, respond to what they say (e.g., "It's great to hear that you've been following the progress of this campaign and also that you're a regular cyclist").

❏ Say briefly what your relationship with the organization is ("I've been involved with this group for the last two years because I ride my bike to work every day and see what the need is").

❏ Briefly describe what you're raising money for and ask if they have any questions about it.

The Ask

❏ Ask for a specific amount of money. ("I'm hoping you can give $50 to this campaign. Would that be possible?")

❏ Wait for an answer. Let them respond.

The Wrap-Up

❏ Answer any follow-up questions.

❏ Describe the process for making their donation.

❏ Thank them for their time and, if appropriate, their donation.

The most important thing is to engage the person you're speaking to. You are calling people you want to cultivate as supporters of your issue and as donors. Make the call as personal as you can. Learn who they are and why they believe in your organization or cause. Be clear and read cues. If a person doesn't want to talk, don't force them to. If a person wants to talk a lot, be clear about how much time you want to spend on a call. It's okay to say, "It's been great talking with you, but I should get going so I can reach more people tonight." If you're polite, people will understand.

The following Phonebank Call Script is an example that you will want to customize to your particular cause and request.

Sample Phonebank Call Script

STRUCTURE OF THE CALL	WHAT TO SAY
Introduction	"Hello, may I speak to Janice Berger? Hi, this is May Hong. I'm a volunteer with the Campaign for Better Bike Lanes. You recently signed a petition asking the city to expand the number of streets that have bike lanes. I'm calling you tonight as part of a membership drive and to update you about our exciting campaign. Do you have a minute?"
If she says no . . .	"When can I call you back?" (Mark on list when to call back and call then.)
If she says she's not interested . . .	Say thank you politely and hang up. (Mark "not interested" on list.)
If she says yes, explain why you're calling and engage her.	"You recently signed a petition to expand the number of streets with bike lanes. Do you bike? Why do you care about this issue?" (Let her answer.) "Glad to hear you're interested. Did you know that the city recently agreed to our proposal?" (Wait for a response.)

STRUCTURE OF THE CALL	WHAT TO SAY
If she doesn't know about it, continue.	"We're very excited by this victory, but (for those who know about the project, you can add, "as you know") the catch is the city can only provide half of the funds needed to create these bike lanes. We agreed to raise the other half, which is $6,000. We're calling you now to ask you to help us reach our goal."
Check in to see if she has any questions.	"Do you have any questions about the project?" (Either answer any questions, or offer to find out the answers if you don't know.)
Make the ask!	"Sounds like you're with us on the need for more bike lanes. We'd like to ask you join us by making a contribution. Would you join us with a gift of $50?" Stop and listen. Pause until they say something.
If they say yes, they'd like to give . . .	"Thank you so much! Can I text you the link to our donation page so you can pay easily and securely right now?"
If they say no . . .	"Thank you for taking the time to talk to me. Can we call you at another time?" (If they give you the impression that they just can't afford to give right now, and you will be doing another fundraising campaign in the future, it's a good idea to ask if you can contact them again. If they aren't interested in your project, just thank them and say goodbye.)

After the call, make notes on the call list about how the call went and what you learned from the person about their involvement and interest in your organization. This will help you continue to build a relationship with them in the future.

Call List

Each phonebanker should receive a list of names with contact information and any other information you have, such as giving history (if applicable), relationship to your group, who knows them, and how you met them or got their name. Make sure there's a column for notes. New or wrong numbers are important to document, along with any relevant information you might learn during a call.

WORKSHEET 7.3
Sample Call List

NAME	PHONE NUMBER	EMAIL	ADDRESS	TIME ZONE	HISTORY	NOTES	RESULT OF CALL	DATE PLEDGED	AMOUNT PLEDGED	DATE RECEIVED	AMOUNT RECEIVED	PAYMENT TYPE
Joe Smith	505-876-1234	joe46@gmail.com	55 Wisteria Lane, Apt 3B Missoula, MT 59801	MT	Gave $25 in 2023	Part of local cycling club	1st attempt: 9/22 Left message 2nd attempt: 9/28 Spoke to daughter; left message with her 3rd attempt: 10/2 Spoke to Joe; just lost his job and can't give right now					
Ray Sung	(413) 444-4444	ray.sung@email.com	123 Fun Lane Portland, OR 97035	PT	Has given $50/year for past 3 years	Former PTA treasurer	1st attempt: 9/22 Asked if we could call back later 2nd attempt: 9/24 Will give $75!	9/24	$75	10/5	$75	Check

It's important to have lists with accurate names and phone numbers so your volunteers don't get too frustrated. However, there will inevitably be a certain percentage of wrong numbers; just make sure your volunteers understand this and know that any new information they learn helps clean up the lists. This is an important job if you want to use these lists again. You also want phonebankers to indicate if they left a message or were told to call back at another time.

It's better to have more names and numbers on your list than you think phonebankers can get through so your volunteers don't run out of numbers to call. Worksheet 7.3 shows what such a call list should look like.

These are names you have collected from your own database, from contacts of your volunteers, or from organizations that were willing to share their lists with you. Your phonebankers will use this list to make their calls and record their results.

Pledge Forms

In the rare instance where someone says they will make a donation but would like you to send them more information by mail, have a pledge form and even just a one-pager that explains what you're raising money for. The Sample Pledge Form provides a template you can use. The phonebanker should ask if the donor would like to pay online via a digital payment app or by check. If by check, be sure to confirm their mailing address. At the end of the evening, you can email, text, or mail any pledge forms to the donor. Make sure to include a separate thank-you message with the pledge form.

Step 6: Make Final Preparations

Once you do these few last things before the phonebank night, you'll be ready:

- Call and text your volunteers as a reminder. Emphasize the importance of the phonebank and let them know there will be a training and snacks. Thank them for agreeing to come.

- Buy, order, or get donations of food or snacks for the night.

- Create any motivational items, like a group "thermometer" poster, to measure the phonebank's success.

- Figure out any other logistics, such as rides or childcare for phonebankers.

SAMPLE PLEDGE FORM

Thank you for your pledge to support our public schools!

Please mail this form with your payment to the address below:

Pledge Amount $_____   Date _____

Name _____

Address _____

City, State, ZIP _____

Phone _____

Email _____

Payment Options:

_____ Check (make payable to "Silver City Public School Foundation")

_____ Credit Card (please fill out the following):

Card Number _____

Expiration Date _____   _____

Signature _____

Date Signed _____

Mail form to
Silver City Public School Foundation,
P.O. Box 5678,
Silver City, NM 80000.

Step 7: Train Volunteers and Carry Out the Phonebank

Your volunteers may be a little nervous at the beginning of the evening. The training you do before the calling begins can help give them concrete tips and confidence to be successful. Remind them that people are often much more receptive to volunteers and to just speak from their heart.

Do a short training at the beginning of the phonebank (about twenty minutes) that includes the following items:

- An icebreaker so that volunteers feel comfortable with each other (something quick, like going around the room saying your name, your favorite snack, and why you're passionate about the cause).

- A description of who you are calling and why, as well as a goal for how much money you want to raise that evening (make this goal exciting but doable).

- A review of materials, including the list of people they'll be calling, the tally sheet, background on what you're raising money for, and the guidance in Phone Tips for Phonebankers.

- Instructions on how to fill out their tally sheet.

- A review of the script, frequently asked questions, and difficult questions.

- Role plays: Have people pair off and spend five or ten minutes each playing the phonebanker. This exercise is important even for people who have participated in phonebanks before. Practice will help everyone get more familiar with the process of calling and with the issues they'll be talking about with prospects.

Tips for Phonebankers

❏ Be friendly and enthusiastic. You can often tell when someone is smiling over the phone, so try smiling as you talk.

❏ Assume the listener's support, be confident, and convey urgency.

❏ Be direct ("We're working to win . . ." not "We're hoping to get . . .").

❏ Adapt the script into your own words; work on sounding conversational.

❏ Listen; draw people out with open-ended questions to discover why they're interested in your issue.

❏ If someone asks you a question you don't know the answer to, be honest and tell them you don't know. If it's an important question, let them know you'll get back to them (and then make a note of it and get back to them yourself or make sure someone else does).

❏ Keep it short and simple. Be clear, concise, and direct. Tell them *why* you're calling at the beginning.

❏ Ask for a specific commitment (a specific amount of money).

❏ Once you make the ask, be silent. Let them think about it and answer. If you need
to, slowly count to twenty in your head to keep yourself from filling the space with
nervous chatter.

❏ Close the deal. Once they make a specific commitment, thank them and secure
the payment method (online or by check). If they need to think about it, ask if
there are any questions you can answer right now. If they still need to think, get a
specific time to call them back (and then follow up).

❏ Thank them for their time.

❏ Remember that practice makes perfect!

Be sure to take good care of your volunteers during the phonebank:

PROVIDE FOOD. Food doesn't have to be elaborate, but some snacks and drinks will
give the volunteers a sense of being cared for. If some volunteers will be coming right
from work, consider providing food they can eat during the orientation.

MAKE IT FUN. Think of ways to create momentum and make the evening enjoyable
for your volunteers. For example, when someone gets a yes, celebrate it—fill up a progress thermometer. Give an award to the person who got the rudest no, the most yeses,
and so on. For in-person phonebanks, you can have people make noise with a noise-
maker every time they get a pledge, or run to the center of the room to ring a bell. With
virtual phonebanks, you can have people share certain emojis in the chat when they get
an answered call, pledge, or other indicators of progressing through the call list.

BRIEFLY CHECK IN WITH PEOPLE EVERY HALF HOUR OR SO. Ask how it's going,
provide pep talks, help solve problems about scenarios that arose, and keep up people's
momentum. Check-ins can be as brief as asking, "Is everything going all right?" so you
don't get people out of their rhythm.

PROVIDE SOME CLOSURE AT THE END OF THE EVENING. Here are some ways to do
that:

- Have people go around and say how it went for them, or check in with them before they leave to find out what their experience was like.

- Give people a chance to briefly share stories about particularly compelling or rude calls.

- Make everyone feel like the night was a big success.

- If you met the evening's goal, celebrate it!

- If you didn't meet the goal, find something positive to highlight in addition to lessons learned for the future.

- If there will be future nights of phonebanking, have people sign up for more shifts or other organizational activities.

If you have the capacity to do so and if you are calling a geographic area that makes this feasible, you might consider having someone actually pick up check or cash donations throughout the night as people make pledges. While this is labor-intensive and requires a volunteer with a car and good people skills, it can be a great way to increase your personal contact with your supporters, and there's a higher chance of actually receiving the check. This especially works if you call people in a specific neighborhood or small town. The in-person contact also allows you to do other quick action steps, such as bringing the person a yard sign to support your issue, getting them to sign a postcard or petition, or collecting other forms of donations, such as food and clothing. Some groups have used this tactic very successfully to augment the effectiveness of their phonebanks.

Step 8: Wrap Up and Send Thank Yous

Once the phonebanking is completed, wrap up this activity with the following tasks:

- Make follow-up calls two weeks later to those who haven't fulfilled their pledge.

- Send thank yous to volunteers within a week of the phonebanking thanking them for their time and giving them a brief report on the results of the evening.

- Send thank yous to donors, ideally within a week of the phonebank.

- If applicable, mail any pledge forms that were requested by the donor with a short note and a reply envelope.

Jewish Voice for Peace (JVP) Phonebank

While JVP currently has a paid staff of about thirty, the group has always had a large team of volunteers involved in fundraising. This continues to the current day. In the early 2000s when it was a mostly volunteer and member-led group, JVP carried out an annual phonebank to ask members to renew their dues and to also consider making an extra donation. Volunteers came into the office for a few nights over two weeks to call through the list, and were able to increase JVP's renewal rate as well as connect with members who had not been as active or in touch recently. In some cases, by reconnecting in this way, members got reinspired to become active again in JVP's political and organizing work.

WORKPLAN

Workplan 7.1 (on the following page) summarizes the key steps necessary to implement this fundraising strategy and an estimated time frame for each step. It is meant to be a template from which to create your own plan and your own timeline. By taking the time to create a plan and timeline, you'll be more organized, more likely to avoid last-minute crises, and ultimately more successful in raising the money you need.

WORKPLAN 7.1
Phonebanks

WHAT	WHO	WHEN (WEEK NUMBER)								DONE
		1	2	3	4	5	6	7	8	
1. Make a plan.										
Make a budget.		×								
Identify potential volunteer roles.		×								
2. Recruit volunteers.		×	×							
3. Get/create lists of people to call.			×	×						
4. Find a location for the phonebank.			×							
Finalize site and date.				×						
5. Prepare materials.					×	×				
6. Make final preparations.										
Call/text volunteers as a reminder.					×	×				
Arrange for food/snacks.					×	×				
Create a visual way to track progress (e.g., a thermometer poster).					×	×				
7. Train volunteers and carry out the phonebank.							×			
8. Wrap up and send thank yous.										
Follow up on pledges made.								×	×	
Send thank yous.								×	×	

8

House Parties

A great way to raise money is the tried-and-true house party. With this strategy, the person hosting the event invites friends and acquaintances to a gathering at their home to learn more about the work of an organization or project. At the party, guests are asked to make a financial contribution. In the weeks leading up to the event, the host sends out invitations, makes calls to encourage people to attend, reminds RSVPs about the party, and asks them to make a contribution even if they can't attend. At the party itself, guests socialize and enjoy food and drinks. When there is a critical mass of people present (and before some guests start to leave), usually about thirty to forty-five minutes after the announced start time of the party, the host and others involved in the project give a brief presentation and answer questions from the guests. The presentation, which should run no longer than about twenty minutes total, includes information about the project for which they're raising money, how much they're trying to raise at the party, and how people can donate. After the program, including some time for Q&A and discussion, guests are encouraged to contribute right away.

House parties can raise several hundred to several thousand dollars. With an invitation list of eighty people from which you would expect about twenty to twenty-five (25 to 35 percent of invitees) to attend, for example, you can expect to raise at least $1,000, and likely closer to $2,000 or more, if you follow the steps in this chapter.

BEST USES

The intimacy of holding an event at someone's home and the fact that guests have some relationship with the host make for a friendly setting where they can get to know the project and give money. House parties are most successful when you have the following ingredients:

- An enthusiastic host—and potentially cohosts—willing to tap into their networks and follow up on the invitation to increase the chances that people will attend

- A strong speaker (this can also be the host or cohost) who can move the audience and make a compelling case for donating

- A list of invitees who support the cause and can make gifts in the amount or range that the host is seeking

- A house that people would enjoy coming to because of its comfort, location, and/ or guests' relationships with the host

THINGS TO CONSIDER

Of all the fundraising strategies described in this book, house parties are among the easiest to organize. They can be carried out by one or two people, in a brief period of time (about six to eight weeks from planning to execution), and without costing much money. The key consideration in choosing a house party over something else is whether you have a large enough list of people to invite who either care a lot about the cause or like the host enough to come even if they don't know the cause or their belief in it isn't particularly strong.

To calculate how much money you'll raise, assume that the average contribution will be between $25 and $500. Some people will also send you money even if they can't attend. Plan that 25 to 35 percent of the people you invite (directly, that is, not through a post on social media) will attend the party.

COSTS

- Food and drink

- Design and printing of any materials you want to have on hand at the party

STEPS TO TAKE

1. Recruit a host (and potentially cohosts) and make a plan.

2. Prepare an invitation list.

3. Prepare and send the invitations.

4. Make follow-up calls and texts.

5. Prepare the agenda, practice the pitch, and hold the party.

6. Send thank yous.

7. Evaluate the event.

As you go through the steps in detail, use the sample workplan at the end of the chapter to create a timeline and task list.

Step 1: Recruit a Host (and Potentially Cohosts) and Make a Plan

Finding a host—and possibly two or more cohosts—is the first step in planning the party. Having more than one host increases the pool of people you can invite and distributes the work of organizing the house party.

An enthusiastic person willing to follow the steps outlined in this chapter is key to the house party's success. If you are planning to organize a series of parties, you may want to have all the hosts gather at the beginning to share tips, learn about what it takes to pull off a successful party, and plan next steps.

House parties usually take four to six weeks to organize, but they can be organized in as little as two weeks. It takes between sixteen and twenty hours of work to plan a successful house party. Here's how that time is generally spent:

- Two to three hours to come up with the program (e.g., speakers or video presentation, who will make the pitch)

- Two hours to prepare the invitation list

- Two to three hours to write, design, and send out the invites

- Four hours to make follow-up calls and texts

- Four to six hours to prepare for and host the house party

- One hour to write thank-you notes

- One hour to evaluate the event

Next, you'll choose a location for the party. House parties can be in-person or virtual. Ideally, house parties should feel like an intimate gathering of friends, but if you don't have enough space in your home to accommodate the number of people you're hoping will attend, you still have a couple of options:

- Consider finding another volunteer(s) to lend their home to the event and also cohost the event with you.

- Find a larger space, like a restaurant's private party room, a church basement, or a workplace conference room. It's important that the space is quiet enough for people to hear a speaker, so a bar or other noisy venue isn't ideal.

Considerations on whether to host an in-person or virtual house party include:

EVENT PLANNING In-person and virtual events have different planning considerations. In-person house parties involve logistics that include hosting and possibly rearranging space, providing food/drink, and planning the in-person experience. Virtual house parties require comfort interacting on a virtual platform to make up for the lack of in-person intimacy through Q&As, chat share-outs, or breakouts.

GEOGRAPHY An in-person event is ideal for participants from a smaller geographic range (county, city, neighborhood). A virtual event helps participants from a wide geographic (statewide or national) join together.

TECHNOLOGY TOLERANCE OF PARTICIPANTS In a world where we're constantly pressured to use our laptops and phones, many participants may not be eager to attend an online house party. This is especially true of people who work remotely. Those who aren't in front of their computers all day may have a higher tolerance for virtual house parties.

PUBLIC HEALTH SAFETY The COVID-19 pandemic brought new awareness of the health risks of meeting with groups of people in indoor and/or crowded spaces. Some hosts and attendees may be immunocompromised or have other hesitations about being exposed to viruses. If this is a consideration for you, consider choosing an outdoor venue and/or requiring or recommending that attendees wear masks.

As the final part of this step, you'll choose a date and time. House parties are usually scheduled for two hours; the best times are weekend afternoons, although weekday evenings can also work. It's important to specify the party's duration to ensure a critical mass of people are there at one time.

Step 2: Prepare an Invitation List

We suggest inviting four times the number of people you want at the party. About a third of the people invited will say that they can come, but in the end only about one-fourth will actually attend. When you make follow-up calls, inviting one hundred people should bring about twenty-five people to a house party; inviting forty people should bring about ten. Tap into your networks! Brainstorm as large of a guest list as possible based on how many people the house can accommodate. For ideas on who to invite, see Resource B on page 188, Who Can You Ask? Tracking down people's emails and phone numbers almost always takes longer than you think, so be sure to budget time for that.

Step 3: Prepare and Send the Invitations

A house party invitation should include the following:

- The date and start and end times

- The address (although sometimes for reasons of security, the host will ask people to RSVP first and send out the exact location only to those who respond)

- A way to RSVP (e.g., by using a link or replying directly to the invitation)

- A link to donate—primarily for those who are unable to attend, but also to receive donations from attendees ahead of time

- A note encouraging the invitees to forward the invitation to friends, if the host is willing to have people they haven't specifically invited attend

- Simple graphics so the invitation is easier to send by text than a more ornate design would be

Use the following Sample House Party Invitation as a guide.

Step 4: Make Follow-Up Calls and Texts

Personal contact by the host is key to making sure people come to the party. It's mainly the host's personal network being invited, and most people will come because they know and trust that person. In addition, people are busy and appreciate the reminder and personal touch of a phone call and/or text. The host should begin making calls and texts two to three weeks before the day of the party.

People who cannot come should still be asked to give a donation. As much as half the money raised from the house party can come from these people if they are asked in a follow-up phone call or text. It's best to ask for a specific amount, saying something like, "I'm hoping you'll consider giving between $50 and $100 to this project." Then write down the amount people commit to on the House Party Tracking Sheet in Worksheet 8.1.

WORKSHEET 8.1
Sample House Party Tracking Sheet

NAME	PHONE	EMAIL	INVITATION SENT?	DATE INVITATION SENT	CONFIRMATION CALL/TEXT MADE?	DATE OF CONFIRMATION CALL/TEXT	ATTENDING?	REMINDER CALL/TEXT MADE?	DATE OF REMINDER CALL/TEXT	PLEDGED	RECEIVED	DATE THANKED	NOTES
Emetra Jones	(601) 222-5353	ejones@email.com	Yes	4/15	Yes	4/22	No			$25	$25	5/5	
Patrick Blackhawk	(601) 222-1234	patrickb@email.com	Yes	4/15	Yes	4/22	Yes	Yes	5/1	$30	Will bring	5/5	Needs child-care for kids 2 and 6 years

Use this worksheet to keep track of invitations sent, follow-up calls made, and whether people are coming. If people are not coming, ask them for a donation and write their pledge in the appropriate column.

See Tips for House Party Turnout Phone Calls for advice on making follow-up phone calls to encourage people to attend the house party.

Tips for House Party Turnout Phone Calls

❑ Get to the point early on in the conversation that you're calling to follow up on the house party invitation. Otherwise, you'll be tempted to have a long chat with your friend and then have a hard time bringing the conversation around to your fundraiser.

❑ Ask directly if they're planning to come to the party.

❑ If they can't come, ask them if they're willing to make a contribution anyway. You can name a specific amount or a range (e.g., between $50 and $250) you'd like them to consider. After you ask for a commitment, be silent and wait for the answer. If you need to, slowly count to twenty in your head to keep yourself from filling the space with nervous chatter.

❑ If they say yes to making a donation, give them specific instructions about how to do so.

❑ Thank your friend for their time.

❑ Carefully record commitments.

It's important to keep track of RSVPs along the way, but even more so as you get closer to the date of your party. If responses are low, you can do more personalized follow-up with your invitee list starting a couple of weeks before the party. The House Party Turnout Call Script illustrates how to structure a follow-up call.

Sample House Party Turnout Call Script

STRUCTURE OF THE CALL	WHAT TO SAY
Opening: You're calling people you know, so be yourself and chat. Be friendly, but make sure to move to the reason for your call.	"Hi, Aunt Rita, this is John. How are you?"
Tell them why you're calling: to follow up on the invitation to your house party.	"Good to hear. Well, as you know, after having a hard time finding a place to live that I can afford, I started getting involved with South Dakotans United. They're a great community organization that's working on affordable housing here. I decided to host a house party to invite my friends and family to learn more and to raise money for South Dakotans United. Did you get my invitation?"
Remind them of the details: tell them when and where the house party is and ask directly if they can come.	"Great. Well, the house party is on Sunday, August 10, from 4:00 to 6:00 in the afternoon. It will be a barbeque in my backyard, and lots of the family will be there. We'll have a short program to explain what South Dakotans United is doing and then you'll have a chance to ask questions and make a donation. Can you join us?"
If they can't come, ask them to make a donation.	"Oh, I'm sorry that it's at the same time as your self-defense class. We'll miss you, but I'd like to ask if you can still make a contribution to South Dakotans United. If so, could you give $60?" (Be silent.) "You can do $40? Great, I'll write that down. Thanks, Aunt Rita, that will make a difference for the campaign. If you'd like, I'll resend you the link to the page where you can make a donation."
If they are planning to come, remind them of the logistics.	"Glad you can make it! Again, the barbeque will be from 4:00 to 6:00 in the afternoon; get here by 4:30 so you can catch the program. Feel free to bring any of your friends!"
Thank them!	"Thanks so much for your time, Aunt Rita, and I'll look forward to seeing you there!"

Step 5: Prepare the Agenda, Practice the Pitch, and Hold the Party

One of the great benefits of house parties is that you can be creative in the type of event you organize, making it culturally relevant and appealing to your guest list. We've heard of and attended parties that featured karaoke, dumpling making, and even a DIY fashion show. It's important to plan the party, the presentation of your project, and especially the fundraising pitch. The first thirty to forty-five minutes are for the guests to arrive, socialize and have some snacks, and check out any materials you have on display. The program should begin no more than forty-five minutes into the party. The following Suggested Program Agenda will give you a sense of how the party will go.

SUGGESTED PROGRAM AGENDA
(20–30 minutes)

(2–5 minutes—Host)	**Introduction:** Welcome and thank people for coming.
(5 minutes—Host or other speaker)	**Why the issue and project are important:** Give a brief presentation on the problem the project or organization is addressing, and why it's important to the speaker as well as to the broader community. Use stories to bring the issue to life.
(5 minutes—Host or other speaker)	**What impact this project will have:** Explain what the goals are and how this project will make a difference.
(5–10 minutes—Speaker continues in this role)	**Questions and answers:** Provide an opportunity to engage the attendees, answer questions, and have a more general discussion.
(5 minutes—Host)	**The fundraising pitch:** Offer concrete ways their support can make a difference. Specify how much you're trying to raise and suggest amounts people should think about giving. After the pitch, give people time to go online and make a donation or fill out a pledge form.
(2 minutes—Host)	**Closing:** Thank everyone for coming and for their support. Invite them to continue eating and socializing.

The Fundraising Pitch

The fundraising pitch should be made after the main presentation(s) and Q&A. Use Resource D on page 190, Tips for Making a Pitch at an Event, to help you create a strong and compelling message.

Immediately after the host makes the pitch, have volunteers stationed around the room for different payment methods: online (provide a QR code on a large poster and have the person making the pitch hold it up so attendees can make a donation from their phones), credit cards, checks, or cash. For people who give by check or cash, ask for their contact information. Give everyone a few minutes to make their donations. Approach people giving via check or cash with a basket to collect the contributions. It is more effective to have someone personally approach people with a basket than to pass the basket around or leave it on a table. This way, guests will more likely make a contribution and will know exactly what to do with it.

Be sure to include an option for people to make a pledge via a contribution slip. Some people will be so moved by the presentation that they decide they want to give a larger amount than they had planned to before hearing more about the cause. But they may need to pledge an amount they'll give later rather than at the party.

Ask everyone who gives by check or cash to fill out the contribution slip and include their contact information and the amount they're giving so that you have a record of who gave what amount. Checks often include people's contact information, but sometimes the contact information is old, and sometimes people give cash and you'll want to have a record of who gave that. This is important so that you can thank people and keep good records for your group.

In addition to asking everyone at the party to make a gift, the house party host(s) should make a monetary donation as well. Hosting the house party is a major contribution. However, for the guests to give money, it makes a difference if the host(s) can say that they gave money and want their friends to join them.

Donations to Political Campaigns

If your house party seeks to raise funds for an electoral campaign, remember that these donations have strict reporting laws, so check the laws of your state and region. The Federal Political Practices Commission requires donors who give more than $250 over the course of an election cycle to report their employer and occupation. It's good practice with any donation of more than $100 to collect this information, and it's even safer if you collect this information for all your donors. Electoral donations are not tax-deductible.

Food and Drink

Refreshments at the house party can be as plain or fancy as you like—whatever fits within your budget. For guests you're especially close to, you can even ask them to bring something to share. The important thing is to have something to eat. Of course, if food is a key feature of the party (and is indicated in the invitation), you'll put more attention there in your planning. If there's time, soliciting favorite local restaurants or stores to donate food will help offset the cost.

Materials

Assemble the following materials to have at the party:

- A poster containing the QR code to the donation page.

- Contribution envelopes, contribution slips, and a basket to collect contributions and pledges.

- Slides and technology to project them (laptop, TV screen or projector, and something to connect the two) if they're being used in the presentation.

- Informational flyers, posters, or photos, to give people an idea of what the group does and to have something to take home to review later (optional). Some materials can be for display only, such as photos, and some materials you should give away to guests.

- If applicable, have swag such as T-shirts, buttons, or books available to sell to guests.

Step 6: Send Thank Yous

Within a week of the house party, send out thank yous to everyone who made a contribution. The host can sign the project's thank yous or send separate ones. It's nice to have the personal touch of a thank you from the host, but if the project is ongoing, it's also important for the group as a whole to begin developing a connection and relationship directly with the donor.

Step 7: Evaluate the Event

Evaluate how the house party went so you can learn from your experience and pass it on to others who may want to do a house party. What went well? What was challenging? How many people came, and how much money did you raise at the party? How much money did you raise from people who didn't come? Did you learn anything that you'd like to pass on to the next house party host or to the organization? Would you feel comfortable coaching someone else to host a house party?

Communities for a Better Environment

In the late 1990s, Stephanie was on the board of an environmental justice organization, Communities for a Better Environment. One of their public awareness activities in the San Francisco Bay Area was to take people on "toxic tours," primarily near the oil refineries in and near Richmond, CA. It was a way to educate the public about the dangers and egregious practices of companies like Chevron, which were polluting whole neighborhoods with the emissions from their refineries. Stephanie and her partner held a house party fundraiser that started with taking people on the toxic tour (which lasted about an hour), after which everyone came to their house for refreshments, socializing, and a pitch for donations. The toxic tour provided a much more dramatic case for financial support than just having someone talk about it at the party, and resulted in not just donations that day but also several people becoming ongoing donors to the organization.

Illinois Coalition for Immigrant and Refugee Rights

A board member at the Illinois Coalition for Immigrant and Refugee Rights decided to host a house party fundraiser for the first time. She had wine and cheese for about fifteen guests, several of whom were from her Filipina network, and others whom she knew from work or who lived in her apartment building. After mingling for the first hour, she showed a short video of the organization and the executive director spoke. The host agreed to announce her own $1,000 commitment that night, and had envelopes and tablets ready to collect donations from the rest of the guests. She raised another $1,000 from the guests in the room that night, totaling $2,000 in new money for the immigrant rights movement.

WORKPLAN

Workplan 8.1 on the following page provides a summary of key steps necessary to implement this fundraising strategy and an estimated time frame for each step. It is meant to be a template from which to create your own plan and your own timeline. By taking the time to create a plan and timeline, you'll be more organized, more likely to avoid last-minute crises, and ultimately more successful in raising the money you need.

WORKPLAN 8.1
House Party

WHAT	WHO	1	2	3	4	5	6	7	8	DONE
1. Recruit a host (and potentially cohosts) and make a plan.										
Recruit hosts.		×								
Choose a date, time, and location of house party.			×							
Make a workplan and budget.			×							
2. Prepare an invitation list.										
Brainstorm as large an invitation list as possible.			×	×						
Track down emails and phone numbers for invitees.			×	×						
3. Prepare and send the invitations.										
Prepare invitation (including RSVP process).				×						
Send out invitations.				×	×					
4. Call and text invitees to follow up.										
Make calls to confirm attendees, ask others to still give.						×	×			
Two days before house party, make reminder calls.								×		
5. Prepare the agenda, practice the pitch, and hold the party.										
Prepare program and pitch.						×	×			
Gather materials needed for the party.							×	×		
Buy and prepare food and refreshments.							×	×		
Hold the party.								×		
6. Send thank yous.									×	
7. Evaluate the event.									×	

9

Community Events

People are social beings, which is probably why special events (or what we're calling community events) are one of the more common fundraising strategies. Community events take advantage of the human desire to come together, have fun, feel part of a community, and also support a cause they believe in. A community event is usually held in a public venue such as a community center, restaurant, hotel, park, street block, or other public space. During the event, attendees mingle, catch up with old friends, meet new people, and look through any materials available about the project. There's often a program to honor someone that may include an emcee, a couple of speakers, some performances, and a fundraising pitch. There can be additional fundraising events within the event framework, such as a silent auction or raffle, which can help raise extra funds.

Your community event can be as creative—and appealing to your target audience—as you want. Just keep in mind that if this is an all-volunteer-led effort, you want to keep any complicated elements to a minimum! Otherwise, you run the risk of spending all of your time preparing for the program and not enough on getting people there and raising as much money up front (from both ticket sales and sponsorships) as possible.

Here are just a few of an almost unlimited number of fun event ideas we've seen:

❏ Talent show

❏ Art expo (with local artists or craftspeople)

❏ Game night or trivia contest

❏ Food tasting or competition

❏ Theme party, such as around a holiday (Halloween, Juneteenth, Purim, Indigenous People's Day, etc.)

The difference between a community event and a house party is that a house party is a more personal gathering of one or two people's networks. The house party relies on the hosts' individual relationships. A community event certainly relies on many people's networks, but the key difference is that it's a larger, public event where supporters of the project or cause come together with people they may or may not already know, and with a goal of reaching as many people as possible. In this chapter, we focus on a more volunteer-run grassroots event as opposed to a high-priced special event that often requires a professional event planner or significant time of a paid staff person. Some of the same principles apply whether you host a larger, high-priced event or a smaller grassroots event, but we concentrate here on how to keep overhead costs down and how volunteers can produce such an event.

BEST USES

Community events are a great fundraising activity if you're trying to do any of the following:

- Raise the visibility of your project.

- Build community, celebrate accomplishments, and deepen relationships with and the commitment of people who have already been involved with your project (as volunteers, donors, or supporters). This relationship building can strengthen other aspects of your project and future potential fundraising work.

- Bring in new money from new people.

- Provide a way for volunteers to learn new skills and get more comfortable with fundraising activities.

Raising large amounts of money is usually not the immediate, primary goal of most community events since there are faster ways of raising money in the short term and events take a lot of work. However, if you're trying to establish your project and you have other community-building goals, community events can be a great way to go.

THINGS TO CONSIDER

Community fundraisers take a lot of work and attention to detail. Before choosing an event as your fundraising strategy, consider whether you have enough (or can find more) volunteers to help carry it out. Depending on how large your event will be, it is good to have a core, committed group of about three to five people and a wider pool of at least another five to ten volunteers. It can be helpful if at least one of the event organizers has had experience planning any kind of event, such as a wedding or commitment ceremony, a family reunion, a big birthday party, or something comparable that would have given them an appreciation for the details and deadlines this kind of undertaking involves.

A successful community event usually takes at least three months to organize; six months is ideal. If your project needs money more quickly and doesn't have upfront money to put into an event (see "Costs"), you might want to switch to a house party or direct personal asks. You may be organizing this as a one-time event, but as with many fundraising strategies, if you can repeat the event year after year, it will become easier and easier to organize (particularly if you keep good records, including evaluations), and you should be able to increase your returns in dollars raised, volunteers recruited, and donors acquired from the event each year. Many organizations that hold annual or semi-annual community events have found that it takes two or three years to smooth out kinks, build a loyal base of attendees, and develop a "tradition" status for the event.

Once the event has been established as a successful affair, a segment of your supporters is likely to return year after year. There will be people who love your event but would not give otherwise. Maybe they love movies or auctions or fun dinners but don't care much about your cause. Some will bring their friends so that new people are introduced to your work. If you follow the steps outlined in this chapter, you can energize your supporters and make a modest amount of money. However, if raising money is your only goal, we don't recommend hosting a community event.

COSTS

You can keep the costs for a community event lower if you get donations of the following items:

- Space for the event
- Tables and chairs

- Food and drink

- Paper goods or place settings

- Equipment (such as a sound system)

- Insurance (liability insurance is sometimes required by the venue)

- Fees and expenses for entertainers or guest speakers

- Childcare

- Invitation design

- Printing for flyers

- Publicity (ads, public service announcements)

- Copying of materials

STEPS TO TAKE

1. Make a plan and budget.

2. Recruit volunteers.

3. Develop the invitation list.

4. Find the event site and set the date.

5. Solicit sponsorships.

6. Design and send invitations.

7. Plan the program.

8. Arrange food, drinks, and other logistics.

9. Publicize the event, make turnout calls, and track progress.

10. Review the event details and hold the event.

11. Evaluate the event and send thank yous.

Use the sample workplan at the end of the chapter to create a timeline and task list.

Step 1: Make a Plan and Budget

The core planning committee sets the goals for the event, makes a workplan and budget, and recruits and coordinates the other volunteers who will help carry out all of the activities required for a successful event. The planning committee should be clear about the goals for the event—fundraising and others—and what resources you have. It's easy for people to get swept up into unrealistic fantasies of what famous person would be great to perform at the event or what kind of food you should have. To avoid going too far afield in dreamland, clarify your goals so that you don't plan an event that loses money and/or doesn't attract the guests you had hoped would attend.

Think about other ways to raise money at the event. Entrance fees and tickets alone do not generally raise the funds you need or tap into attendees' giving potential. Because many groups have found that ticket sales represent such a small portion of the funds they're able to raise from their events, they've gone to a free admission approach, putting more effort into raising money through sponsorships and other activities listed below. We mention it here as an option to consider but generally don't recommend it. When someone has bought a ticket to an event, they're far more likely to show up than if they haven't. Also, even though ticket sales rarely bring in as much money as you need—and sometimes barely cover the costs of producing the event—they're a source of income that can make a difference in how much money you raise. Having said that, make ticket prices as affordable as possible and even offer discounts to make sure no one is turned away because they can't afford a ticket.

Community fundraisers are versatile events because you can easily build other forms of fundraising into them, such as the following:

- Making a pitch at the event

- Raffles

- Silent auctions

- Event sponsorship (see Resource H on page 195 for more on sponsorships)

- Table sponsors

Later chapters describe raffles and auctions in detail. These extra fundraising activities also allow you to tap into people who may not attend the event but can provide support through these other mechanisms. That means that you should sell raffle tickets and begin publicizing silent auctions far before the actual event to reach the fundraising potential of these extra activities. These strategies are a perfect project for a subcommittee of volunteers to coordinate. Make sure there's clear, consistent communication among the committees organizing these auxiliary fundraising strategies and the volunteers who are soliciting sponsorships and other in-kind items for the event so that they're not asking the same vendors or people for donations twice.

Decide if you want a host committee or sponsors for the event. A host committee is usually a group of people willing to lend their name, invite their friends, buy a ticket, and attend the event. It's a way to build the audience and give some measure of credibility to your project or cause. It's best to recruit a host committee early on in the process so their names can be included on the invitation. Usually, committee members are asked to contribute financially to the event even if they can't attend.

The key to a successful community event is good planning. Creating a detailed workplan on the front end will save you many headaches in the long run. Because tasks carried out mainly by volunteers are so important to successful events, it's important that your workplan specify the point person and other volunteers for every task or series of problems that may come up on each project. Even then, expect some crises, such as a speaker or performer who gets sick the day before the event or a typo that advertises the wrong date for the event.

Consider organizing your volunteers into committees to carry out the range of tasks required. You might have a committee that works on the program (speakers, location, food, and so on); another committee that works on the invitation and publicity to get people to attend; and a third committee that works on increasing the money raised by recruiting sponsors, holding a raffle, or including a silent auction. The core planning committee should develop the overall workplan that sets goals, parameters, and as much detail as possible for the project committees. Generally, err on the side of more detail rather than less since it's better to have a conversation on the front end about differing approaches than after something has been implemented differently than you envisioned. For example, don't send the program committee off to figure out who the entertainers and speakers will be without defining some parameters. If the planning committee's vision is for the program to have community members perform and be the key speakers, the program committee needs to know it so that they don't go off and recruit the local, flashy politician who is a good speaker but doesn't represent the values of your project or organization.

To decide whether a community event is the right activity for your group, consult the Planning Example for a Community Event. Use this sample worksheet with your planning committee to come up with fundraising goals, goals besides raising money, and resources. Then use the steps in the chapter and sample workplan to make a detailed plan.

PLANNING EXAMPLE
for a Community Event

What are our fundraising goals?

❏ How much do we need to raise?

$7,500 (Need to raise total of $10,000—costs of $2,500 to reach goal of $7,500)

❏ How can we raise money from people/places that would not give otherwise?

Table sponsorships—local businesses, current donors, and/or close friends and family, nonprofit ally organizations

❏ Can we get in-kind donations for the event?

Yes. Ask Rosi's Diner, Taqueria Cancun, JJ's Café. Brainstorm with volunteers.

❏ In addition to ticket sales, what are other ways to raise money at the dinner?
  - ❑ Fundraising pitch
  - ◼ Raffle
  - ◼ Silent auction
  - ❑ Table sponsorship
  - ◼ Other: *Sponsor others to come*

Do silent auction—we know artists who might donate work. Instead of raffle, ask people who can't come to sponsor others.

What are our goals besides raising money? Do we want to:

❏ Increase our project's visibility? Celebrate victories? Thank and motivate people?

❏ Increase volunteer commitment, fundraising skills, other skills?

Arts expo is in 6 months—we want to increase visibility of our arts group.

Need volunteers to plan arts expo—recruit 15 volunteers to help plan dinner so that at least 5 can help with expo. Especially train on fundraising.

Need artist submissions—insert call for art submissions into event invitation.

What resources do we have?

❏ How much money do we have up front?

$500—need another $2,000

❏ Who can we ask for money?
We have a list of 600 people who have attended our art expos in the last 3 years. Our event and arts expo planning teams should also brainstorm lists of others we should invite.

❏ How much time do we have to plan the event?
3 months

❏ Who can we recruit to help plan and run the event?
20 volunteers from last year's expo. Call and recruit them to help with fundraising event for this year's art expo. Also, ask past volunteers for suggestions of other people who may be willing to help.

❏ Other resources: *Artists who can donate work*

Step 2: Recruit Volunteers

Community events depend on the enthusiasm and commitment of volunteers. A community event can be a nice entry point for someone to learn new skills, find out more about the project, and become invested in the future of the project. The skills you need to produce a community event can translate very well to other work your project does, such as organizing a speaking event, putting on a rally, recruiting people to a public meeting to make demands of a city council, and so forth.

Here are some ideas of what volunteers can do:

- Find the event venue.

- Send invitations to and follow up with their friends, family, and networks.

- Solicit sponsorships.

- Sell tickets to the event.

- Serve as event photographer.

- Make food.

- Serve food and drink.

- Help with room setup and cleanup.

- Recruit performers and speakers.

- Be a performer or speaker.

- Do the fundraising pitch.

- Collect donations after the pitch.

- Write thank-you letters to people who give money.

See Resource A on page 187, the Volunteer Recruitment Form, for help with recruiting volunteers. Once you have your volunteer crew, focus on training and supporting them and being thoughtful about how they like to work and how they can plug in. Troubleshoot if problems arise. It's useful to have benchmarks in your workplan to measure how progress is going and to help adjust plans if needed.

Step 3: Develop the Invitation List

With your volunteers, brainstorm a list of friends, family, coworkers, neighbors, and acquaintances who might be interested in learning more about your project and who might enjoy coming to a community event. (Use Resource B on page 188, Who Can You Ask?, to help brainstorm whom to invite.) You'll need to send invitations to between two hundred and three hundred people if you want fifty people to come to your event. This does not include posting on social media, where hundreds more may see the invitation, but, because it's not a direct ask, you won't get as large a response as with email or even snail mail. You may want to invite people who live in another state or can't attend for some other reason but may be willing to make a contribution anyway.

Step 4: Find the Event Site and Set the Date

Try to get the space for your event donated or rented at a low rate. Especially if this is the first event you're organizing, it's not wise to invest a lot of money on the front end. Being somewhat flexible about the date of your fundraiser can allow you to take advantage of any free or low-cost spaces.

Consider a location that your supporters will find convenient and comfortable. If your project works on women's or gender-related issues, see if there are any women's centers or YWCAs with available space. If your project is based in a particular racial/ethnic community, find a location that is accessible and safe for your potential guests. As soon as you set a date, send out a "Save the Date" email to your closest supporters and volunteers.

Think about all the arrangements you'll need to make for the event and what types of facilities will be required. Considerations might include the following:

- Is there a kitchen where you can heat up donated food or have volunteers help cook food?

- Do you need to provide childcare? If so, have a child-friendly room nearby, rather than just a corner in the event room, so the kids can play without disrupting the program.

- Is the space you're considering accessible to people with disabilities? This could include but is not limited to issues like public transit/parking, entrances and exits, seating, ASL interpretation, flashing lights, strong scents, food allergies, and restrooms. You want to make sure that everyone in the community is welcome.

- Are there enough tables and chairs for your event, or do you need to borrow some?

- Does the place already have a sound system or will you need to borrow or rent one?

- Does the venue require you to have liability insurance?

If liability insurance is required, you have a couple of options depending on your group. If you're an established nonprofit organization with an office, you might already have a policy for liability insurance to which you can add a rider that covers you for the day of the event. If you're an all-volunteer group that's not part of a nonprofit organization, you can sometimes get coverage for liability insurance by using the homeowner's insurance policy of a group member. Check with the person's insurance company. If no one owns a home, find out if the venue itself can cover you under their liability insurance, even if it means charging you something for that coverage.

Step 5: Solicit Sponsorships

While not required for a successful event, most events that raise significant amounts of money are able to do so because of the support of businesses and individual donors who are willing to make donations that are larger than the price of a ticket. It's best to solicit sponsorships early on in the process of organizing an event so that you can include the names of sponsors in your invitiation and other publicity materials. It also allows you to track how you're doing financially to ensure you meet your fundraising goals and, if you're falling short, to identify other ways to make up the gap.

See Resource H on page 195 for sample language to use with potential sponsors as well as examples of sponsorship levels and benefits.

Step 6: Design and Send Invitations

The invitations can be simple, but if you have a volunteer with design skills, this is the time to let them shine! Just be sure to include the key information in the invitation: what, where, and when; directions to the venue; and the link, number, or email to reply. If you've identified a speaker, performer, or honoree, publicize this on the invitation to entice prospective attendees. It's also critical to have several people proofread the invitation to catch and correct any errors before sending it out.

Consider bringing volunteers together to send out the invitations. Each volunteer would send individual emails to their lists (or a group email), but doing this process together builds connections among team members. It's a great way for volunteers to get to know one another, learn more about the project, and help get some concrete work done. Ask volunteers to add a couple of sentences to the invitations in their own words to add a special personal touch. Here is a sample fundraising event invitation for a peace and justice organization in Missouri:

A Musical Journey of Peace
benefiting Peace Economy Project

— Guests —

Rick Burkhardt   Charlie King
Good Trouble

JOIN US!
05 Sept, 2024 | 7:00 PM
Tickets $20 - $50, purchase online at
peaceeconomyproject.org

Eden Seminary | 475 E. Lockwood Ave, St Louis, MO

We've curated a lineup of musicians whose artistry and passion for peace align with the core mission of the Peace Economy Project: to redirect military spending toward human needs.

Step 7: Plan the Program

The program is where you introduce your project's mission and accomplishments. You can include one or two speakers who are inspirational, represent your project, and can connect with your audience. The program is also an opportunity to have presenters and/or performers who will resonate with your audience and convey the image and values of your project. It's ideal if one of your planning committee members has seen the presenter and can attest that they're a good fit for your event.

The emcee can make or break an event. Consider the tone you want to convey at your event and choose an emcee to match that tone. If you want your event to be solemn and inspirational, don't choose your friend who's an aspiring comedian. If you want your emcee to be snappy and move the program along, don't choose the wonderful but long-winded community activist who always tells lengthy stories of how things were back in the day. Someone from your coordinating committee should prepare the emcee by being clear about the tone you're trying to convey, familiarizing them with the program and the flow of the room, and conveying any talking points they should use. Make sure your emcee has a written, detailed agenda and talking points for the program, including any bios for performers and pronunciation keys for people's names. Plan to have someone from the coordinating committee near the stage during the program part of the dinner in case the emcee has questions or unforeseen circumstances arise, such as a performer who arrives late or the need for last-minute logistical announcements.

Step 8: Arrange Food, Drinks, and Other Logistics

Good food—and enough of it—is very important to a community event's success. People who are happy and full are much more likely to give money and walk away feeling good about the evening and your project than people who are hungry throughout the event. So don't skimp on the food!

As with other items for the event, the more you can get donated, the better. Here are some tips for soliciting donations of food and drink:

- Make a list of restaurants and caterers that you and other volunteers frequent or have used. It's much easier to get a food donation from a restaurant that recognizes you as a regular customer.

- Call and, if you're soliciting a restaurant, consider going in person at slower times of the day. Introduce yourself and your project, ask who you should speak to about making donations, and find out how to follow up on your request.

- Consider sending a simple email explaining your project and the purpose, date, and time of your event, and clearly asking for a food donation. If you have any print materials about the event or your request, you can leave them with the manager.

- Be sure to specify if you'll display the name of their restaurant or catering service at the event, give them recognition in the program, or otherwise bring their business good publicity.

- Some grocery stores will also donate food and sometimes drinks. If you are considering serving alcohol, find out if the venue allows it and if you need a liquor license.

It's useful to develop a "run of show" with the timing of each part of the event for anyone who will be involved in the day of activities. This helps everyone picture the event, identify items that haven't yet been taken care of, and clarify roles needed for the day. You may want to get your committees to draw up a detailed plan for each of their pieces and then create a master plan for the flow of the dinner. Be as detailed as you possibly can. Here are some examples of things to include:

- How can people get to the venue using public transit? Where will drivers park?

- How is the food arriving at the site? Is it being delivered? By whom? Is it being picked up? By whom?

- Will food need to be reheated? Where and by whom? Does the food need to be kept warm? How will that happen?

- How will registration or ticket sales happen? What lists need to be set up beforehand, and what information should they contain? How will volunteers get the lists they need?

- Who is working with the emcee? Who is the timer for the speakers? Who will be managing the performers or speakers?

- Who is doing the fundraising pitch? Who will be going around the room to collect donations?

By thinking through these details ahead of time, you can readjust the flow of the event plan as needed. You'll also have enough time to recruit volunteers and prepare people who have roles during the event, such as your speakers and emcee.

When creating the run of show for the event, include clear logistics and schedule food donation pick-ups.

Volunteers can also donate food (cooked or just ingredients) and drinks to the event. The event can also be a potluck, which is a good way for volunteers to participate and share. Another option is for a committee of cooks to have a food budget and cook the meal. In that case, be sure that the cooks have the appropriate facilities to prepare and heat food. Once the menu is set, make it clear to attendees whether and/or which dietary restrictions can be accommodated.

Have a place in the RSVP form for the respondent to indicate whether they'll need childcare and for what ages; also ask volunteers doing turnout calls to ask about childcare needs and the children's ages. Make sure there is a separate room for childcare if needed, and have appropriate toys available.

Some other considerations: Who will unlock and lock the event venue? Where do you put the trash at the end of the night? The more you plan ahead and make these arrangements, the smoother your evening will go.

Step 9: Publicize the Event, Make Turnout Calls, and Track Progress

Aside from the formal invitation, you can publicize the event more broadly. Craft a simple email that explains your cause, makes the event look appealing, gives clear logistics, and indicates an easy way to reply. Forward this announcement to appropriate lists and encourage others to forward it as well. You may want to publicize the event through other free or low-cost avenues; Resource G on page 194 covers some ways to help you get the word out. Always keep in mind, however, that the personal contact of a phone call or text is the most effective way to get people to turn out to any event.

Making turnout calls, texts, and voice memos is one of the most important steps. There's no use in having a fantastic program, the best raffle items, and delicious food if people don't actually come to the event. The most effective way to make sure people come is to make follow-up phone calls, text, or send voice memos to the people who received invitations and to those who bought tickets in advance. This personal contact can make your event stand out, help someone understand your project better, and allow you to count on at least a certain number of attendees. People are much more likely to attend if they actually purchase their ticket ahead of time, so as much as possible, encourage the person to send in their reply along with a donation.

The goal of turnout phone calls is to get the event on people's radar, ask them to pay for and send in the money for their tickets ahead of time, and get a sense of how many will be coming. Even if you make turnout calls a couple of weeks in advance, some people will wait to buy tickets until the last few days beforehand and others will just show up on the day of. It's important for you to estimate how many people you think will attend so that you can have the right amount of food.

Another important goal of the phone call, text, or voice memo is to ask people who won't be able to attend to make a contribution nonetheless. You can ask them to sponsor other community members to attend the fundraiser or to make a straightforward contribution. As you make phone calls, consider Five Tips for Event Turnout Phone Calls.

FIVE TIPS FOR EVENT TURNOUT PHONE CALLS

❏ Be friendly; introduce yourself and explain why you're calling.

❏ Ask directly if people will come to the event.

❏ If they can attend, sign them up and ask them to donate ahead of time. If they can't come, ask them to make a contribution to the project.

❏ After you ask for a commitment, be silent and wait for their answer. If you need to, slowly count to twenty in your head to keep yourself from filling the space with nervous chatter.

❏ Carefully record commitments—including those who say they will attend, those who say no, and those who say no but are willing to make a donation.

Here's an example of a call following up on a dinner invitation:

Janet: *Hi, my name is Janet and I'm a parent with Schools for All Tennesseans, SAT. May I please speak to Dennis?*

Dennis: *This is Dennis.*

Janet: *Hi, Dennis. As you may know, next month is the anniversary of the Supreme Court decision in Brown v. Board of Education essentially outlawing segregation in schools. SAT is hosting a celebration and fundraising dinner at Creekside Elementary School. Did you get our invitation?*

Dennis: *Yes, I think I received something in an email from the PTA.*

Janet: *Great! So you have kids who go to Creekside?*

Dennis: *Two of them.*

Janet: *Well, then you know that the school is cutting after-school programs, which makes it real hard for parents who have to work.*

Dennis: *Yeah, I'm not sure what to do with mine.*

Janet: *Well, SAT is going to the school board to give them a piece of our mind, but we need community members to join us and also to come to our fundraising dinner. Our dinner is on Saturday, May 15th, from 5:00 to 7:00 P.M. at Creekside. Should be a lot of fun. Can you join us?*

Dennis: *Saturday, hmm. I think we can do it. Sure.*

Janet: *Great, I'll sign you up right now. How many people from your family should I sign up?*

Dennis: *Me, my two kids, and their grandmother.*

Janet: *Okay, that's four seats. Tickets are $35 for each adult, and $7 for kids, so that totals $84. How would you like to pay?*

Dennis: *Well, that's a lot.*

Janet: *Yes it is, but we're investing in our kids' programs and future.*

Dennis: *Well, I suppose I can do that. I'll pay when we get there.*

Janet: *Actually, it helps us a lot in our preparations if you could make your donation ahead of time. I can email or text you a link to our online donation page or you can send a check in the mail. Which of those works best for you?*

Dennis: *Oh, okay. I'll go donate online right now. I just pulled up the link from the PTA email.*

Janet: *Great! It was nice speaking with you and thank you for your time! I look forward to meeting you. See you at the celebration on Saturday, May 15th!*

Dennis: *See you then. And thank you for all your work.*

If Dennis can't come to the dinner, Janet asks him to donate anyway:

Dennis: *No, I'm sorry, May 15th is my mother's birthday and we're all going out to dinner.*

Janet: *Oh, I'm sorry that you can't join us. We'd love to have you there in spirit anyway. You can sponsor two community members to join us that night. Tickets are $35 each. Could you sponsor two community members at $70?*

Dennis: *Well, I don't think I can do $70, but I'll do one ticket at $35.*

Janet: *Thanks, that would be great. I'll write that down. We can take credit card over the phone, checks by mail, or online donations. Information on how to donate can be found in the email invite you received. Can we call you when we speak at the school board?*

Dennis: *Definitely. I'd like to give them a piece of my mind, too.*

Janet: *Okay, we'll call you. Have a nice birthday celebration! Good night!*

To ensure the absolute best turnout, make a round of reminder calls to everyone who has RSVPed. Keep it short and simple. Tell them you're making sure they have the details—the specific time, logistics, and any tips on things like transit and parking options.

Use the tracking sheet in Worksheet 9.1 to track who you sent invitations to, your follow-up calls, who will be coming, how much money they commit to giving, and whether their donation has been received.

It's important to check in with your team regularly as you conduct turnout calls to see how many confirmed RSVPs you have and how many tickets have been purchased. You can do this on a weekly basis initially and as the event gets closer, you can have a quick check-in daily. This can ease anxiety about whether or not you'll meet your fundraising and attendance goals, and if you're not getting the response you need, you can encourage team members to make more follow-up calls.

WORKSHEET 9.1
Sample Event Invitation, Turnout, and Donation Tracking

NAME	PHONE	EMAIL	ADDRESS	DATE INVITATION SENT	DATE OF CONFIRMATION CALL/TEXT	ATTENDING?	PLEDGED	RECEIVED	DATE THANKED	NOTES
Ernest Hum	(601) 222-5353	ernestm@email.com	15 Fifth Ave.	7/17	7/28	No	$50	$50	8/12	
Joan Swan	(601) 222-1234	joan@email.com	316 Aspen	7/17	8/1	Yes				Janice's sister

Step 10: Review the Event Details and Hold the Event

Materials

Make a checklist of all the materials you need for the community event. Double- and triple-check the list before the event. Here are some of the items you may need:

- Guest lists with indications of who has replied and who has prepaid

- Cash and change for ticket purchases at the door

- Pens for registration and writing checks

- Signs to direct people (to the restrooms, to the coat room, to childcare, and so on)

- Tables and chairs

- Scissors, stapler, and tape (duct and Scotch)

- Flyers and other informational materials about the issue and project

- Markers: regular and permanent (in case you have to make signs for outside)

- Name tags

- Reply envelopes, contribution cards, and baskets for collecting check and cash donations after the pitch

- Credit card readers if you're accepting donations by credit card

- Poster with QR code that links to donation page

- Computers and/or tablets for people to pay for ticket and/or make a donation

- Eating utensils, plates, napkins

- Decorations

- Ladder to help hang things up

- Other _____

Space Layout

Plan the physical layout of the event space and how people will move around the space. Where will people register? Plan to set up the registration table so that everyone arriving has to sign in and pay for their tickets if they haven't already done so, and make sure there's enough room for people waiting to register.

Where will people mingle before the programming kicks off? Is the food served sit-down or buffet style? If it's buffet style, how do you want people to line up and get food? This can take a lot of time if not done right. Do you want to have servers plate people's food? The advantage of this is that you can manage portions, but the disadvantage is that it's sometimes slower. If people serve themselves, it's much faster to arrange the buffet table so that a line can go along each side of the table.

Run of Show

Next, plan out the run of show, which is an outline of how the evening will go. Here's a sample run of show for a fundraising event (for this example, we're assuming someone is being honored, but that's not a requirement for a successful event):

6:00	Guests begin arriving. They mingle, get drinks, and find a place to sit. Volunteers sell last-minute raffle tickets (if a raffle is part of the event).
6:30	Food is served.
7:00	The program begins. The emcee welcomes everyone, introduces the project or organization very briefly, and then introduces the first speaker or performer.
7:05	The performance, speech, or video is presented.
7:10	The emcee introduces someone directly impacted by the work or deeply involved in some way with the project or organization. This person describes the project and shares a personal story about why they're involved and why the issue is important to them.
7:20	The emcee or another speaker introduces the honoree and presents the award. The honoree speaks about the issue and importance of this project.
7:35	A community leader thanks the honoree, reinforces the importance of the project, makes a fundraising pitch, and asks people to donate or pledge at this time.
7:40	Volunteers circulate around the room with baskets to collect contributions.
7:45	The emcee or another speaker holds a raffle drawing (optional).
7:50	The emcee closes the program, thanks everyone, and tells people to stay around to mingle. If you're able to do this, it can be very inspiring to have a couple of people add up the amount that was donated during the pitch and announce it before the close of the program.
7:50–8:15	Guests mingle and have coffee, tea, and perhaps dessert.

It's important to keep track of time and to keep the program moving. If you're running too late, people will start trickling out before the fundraising pitch, and the event may fizzle instead of ending on a high note. The emcee plays a key role in moving the program along. Let all the speakers and performers know in advance how much time they'll have and that someone will cue them when they get close to the end of their time. Nevertheless, plan ahead for the inevitable extra time people will take. Have the cue person sit discreetly in the front, in easy view of the speaker, and hold up signs indicating as the speaker's time limit approaches: "3 minutes," "1 minute," "30 seconds," "Stop."

The Laotian Dance Auction

According to Torm Nompraseurt of the Asian Pacific Environmental Network (APEN), the Laotian Dance Auction is a special event that is very popular in the Laotian community. During the dance, which sometimes includes raising money for a particular cause or family in need, people enjoy food and drink and buy dance rounds in honor of friends, family, and other community members throughout the night. The dance might be held to celebrate the Khmu New Year or Valentine's Day, to commemorate an organization's anniversary, or to support the Lao Temple. A live band plays songs that people request—and pay for. The more you pay for your song, the earlier it gets played and the more respect it shows to the person to whom you're dedicating it. Also, if a song is bought and dedicated to you, you usually return the favor and buy a round for that person. A good emcee keeps the crowd excited and the bids flying. Sometimes the dance purchasing can become so frenzied that there isn't enough time to play all the songs before the party ends. In that case, the band might play shortened versions of some songs to make sure they all get played. In addition to the dance round bidding, the event raises money through admission and by selling flowers, food, and drinks. Like many events, the key to its success is personal relationships. If the organizers of the dance have good relationships with the leader of a clan, the whole clan will come to the dance. It's not unusual to have two hundred to four hundred people attend a Laotian Dance Auction, and ones that celebrate the Lao New Year have attracted as many as two thousand attendees. Income from the songs "purchased" by attendees generally ranges from $2,000 to $4,000.

The Fundraising Pitch

During the fundraising pitch, someone tells a brief and often very personal story that illustrates why the cause or organization is so important and asks people to make a gift above and beyond what they paid to attend. At that point, QR codes and links are shared so people can donate online, envelopes and pens are provided for people to write checks, a container is passed around for cash and checks, and sometimes credit card readers are available for volunteers to collect credit card donations.

Ask a volunteer or member of your project who is comfortable speaking in front of a crowd to make a fundraising pitch. The person doing the pitch should talk briefly about why the cause is so important to them, explain what the group will be able to do with additional support, ask very clearly for a donation, and name the goal ("Tonight, we want to raise $X"). Then, they should pause to make sure people know how they can donate (online, credit card, check, or cash) and give them enough time to do so. See the tips on delivering the pitch in Resource D.

Womenade

A group of women turned potlucks into pots of gold for unhoused residents of Washington, DC. Dr. Amy Kossoff, a doctor at a shelter, spent thousands of her family's dollars helping her very poor patients buy medicines, eyeglasses, and other necessities. When her friends found out how much she was spending, they decided to help the cause and created Womenade. Once or twice a year, the women held a huge potluck dinner. Each woman brought a dish to share and also donated $35. The money went into an account that Dr. Kossoff used to help her clients make ends meet. These dinners became so popular that they eventually raised thousands of dollars and were replicated all over the country for many different causes.

Loteria

Stephanie's nieces attended a bilingual Spanish-English public school in San Francisco called Buena Vista. The students' parents used to organize an annual fundraising event called Loteria, which is based on the popular Mexican bingo game of that name. Whole families attended, both for the fun of playing loteria and for the delicious potluck dinner. From a combination of fees charged to play the game and tickets to the dinner itself, this event raised several hundred dollars each year. While not a huge sum, it was also an opportunity for community building among the families. And because the event was organized by parents and the school donated the space, there were very few expenses.

Step 11: Evaluate the Event and Send Thank Yous

Evaluating your event will give you important information about whether you met the goals you set for it, as well as areas for improvement for future events. Here are some questions to ask:

- Did you meet your financial goal, both gross (that is, the total income from the event) and net (what was left after expenses)?

  - How many people attended the event, and did you reach your goal for the number of attendees?

  - Did you recruit enough volunteers to make the workload reasonable for each one?

- If it's important to your group: Did you increase your visibility with a targeted constituency or an influential decision-maker?

- Are your key leaders who worked on this project excited to work together on other fundraising or non-fundraising projects?

- Are there things that you would change about the community event planning or logistics if you did this again?

Even if you didn't meet your fundraising goals, it's just as important to analyze why. The successes and mistakes you make are important lessons to pass on. Your team should also recommend whether this event should be repeated—if not, why not, and if so, how. If you decide to do a community event again, all your records—evaluation records, donor records, workplans, invitation originals, and so on—will make it much easier for people doing an event like this another time, and will probably help them bring in more money as well. Also, your volunteers have worked hard to put on this community event, so draw out all the successes and celebrate.

Thank yous go a long way toward deepening people's commitment to your project and making them want to return for more and continue being supporters. Send thank yous within a week or two of the event to all the volunteers who worked on the event and everyone who attended.

WORKPLAN

Workplan 9.1 summarizes the key steps necessary to implement this fundraising strategy and an estimated time frame for each step. It is meant to be a template from which to create your own plan and your own timeline. By taking the time to create a plan and timeline, you'll be more organized, more likely to avoid last-minute crises, and ultimately more successful in raising the money you need.

WORKPLAN 9.1
Community Events

WHAT	WHO	1	2	3	4	5	6	7	8	9	10	11	12	DONE
1. Make a plan and budget.														
Plan the overall vision and goals for the event.		×												
Make a budget.		×	×											
Make a workplan.		×	×											
Decide on which fundraising activities to include (e.g., sponsorships, auction).		×	×											
Identify potential volunteer roles.		×	×											
2. Recruit volunteers.														
Match volunteers with roles and responsibilities.		×	×	×										
Provide training if needed.			×	×										
Check in and provide ongoing support.				×	×	×	×	×	×	×	×	×	×	
3. Develop the invitation list.														
Brainstorm the invitation list with volunteers and others.			×	×										
4. Find the event site and set the date.														
Decide on site needs: childcare room, kitchen, size, etc.			×	×										
Contact and visit potential sites.			×	×										
Finalize the site and date.					×									
5. Solicit sponsorships.				×	×	×	×	×						
6. Design and send invitations.														
Design the invitation (including establishing the RSVP process).					×	×								
Send the invitations.						×	×							
Have a "recruitment" party.								×						

WHAT	WHO	WHEN (WEEK NUMBER)												DONE
7. Plan the program.														
Design the program agenda.					×	×								
Recruit and prep speakers and performers.					×	×	×	×						
Arrange the sound system.									×	×				
Orchestrate the fundraising pitch.											×	×		
8. Arrange food, drink, and other logistics.														
Get food and drink donations; decide whether to cook or cater.						×	×	×	×					
Buy/borrow utensils and other necessary items.											×	×		
Decide whether childcare is necessary and prepare.										×	×			
Make a plan for getting into and closing up the event site.											×	×		
Make any other needed arrangements.										×	×	×		
9. Publicize the event, make turnout calls, and track progress.														
Sell tickets and get contributions from invitees.							×	×	×	×	×	×	×	
Publicize the event through neighborhood forums, flyers, local paper, and so on.									×	×	×	×	×	
10. Review the event details and hold the event.														
Do a minute-by-minute breakdown and run-through with key people.											×			
Set up and clean up.												×		
Hold the event.												×		
11. Evaluate the event and send thank yous.														
Evaluate and celebrate with the volunteer team.												×		
Document the event.												×		
Send out thank yous.												×		

10

Pledge-Raising Events

Pledge-raising events are well known and utilized for fundraising and publicity for a range of causes. The best-known ones are walk-a-thons or bike-a-thons for medical research on HIV/AIDS, leukemia, lymphoma, and breast cancer, for example. Organized by professional fundraisers or organizations that specialize in producing them, these events require up to a year of advance planning and are relatively complicated to organize. However, you can adapt these events for a smaller organization or project, and they can be organized by a dedicated team of volunteers in a much shorter period of time.

Pledge-raising events can be actual physical activities, as just described, or virtual ones. Before the scheduled day of the event, your volunteer fundraising team asks people they know to donate as a way of supporting both the cause and the team's involvement in the event.

Here are some examples of pledge events:

- Bowl-a-thons

- Read-a-thons for kids

- Dance-a-thons

- Individual or small-group bike-a-thons or walk-a-thons

- Speech-a-thons (where a group of people speak, debate, or read speeches of famous people, such as Dr. Martin Luther King Jr., for a certain period of time)

- Clean-a-thons (where you recruit volunteers to clean, say, the home of a senior)

- Protest-a-thons (where people seek pledges for their participation in a protest)

BEST USES

Pledge-raising events of all kinds are fun to participate in, and people who might otherwise be reluctant to ask for money find it easier to approach someone to sponsor their participation. Pledge-raising events are a good community-building activity as well, as people join together to have fun and raise money at the same time. For some people, the physical challenge of a pledge event is a motivating factor in their decision to participate; raising money for a good cause may be secondary.

Bowl-a-thons and dance-a-thons in particular work well for several reasons. First, they can be carried out by a small group of volunteers. Second, they can be inexpensive to put on. Third, they're not dependent on good weather. Fourth, you don't have the complexities of getting permits, disrupting traffic, and dealing with issues of safety that are required for many walks, runs, and bike-riding events.

THINGS TO CONSIDER

You may have no problem recruiting ten of your friends to participate in a bowl-a-thon or dance-a-thon, but their willingness to ask people to pledge support for their efforts is what brings in the money.

While pledge-raising events are straightforward and not as complicated to pull off as other events, the tasks that your fundraising team is required to do involve a higher level of commitment than some other strategies. For example, a participant in a pledge-raising event must identify and solicit their friends, family, and others in their networks for a donation, as well as participate in the activity on the day of the event. So it's important to support and motivate your team of volunteers to make sure they ask for donations, collect them before or after the event, and if possible, recruit people they know to become participants who also ask for donations. The lead time required for a small-scale pledge event like a bowl-a-thon or dance-a-thon is about two months. Plan on at least twice that much time for a walk-a-thon, bike-a-thon, or swim-a-thon that requires finding a location and possibly getting permits.

COSTS

- Space rental and/or permits
- Refreshments for participants
- Silly prizes for participants (for example, with a bowl-a-thon, "Most Gutters")

MATERIALS NEEDED FOR VOLUNTEERS

- Tips on how to ask for money to sponsor your pledge-raising activity

- A copy of Resource B on page 188, Who Can You Ask?

- Spreadsheet or form to track pledge solicitation

- Sample solicitation letter

- Fact sheet or brief description of the project

STEPS TO TAKE

1. Make a plan.

2. Recruit volunteers.

3. Secure space rental and permits (if applicable).

4. Conduct a training or orientation for volunteers, and start asking for donations and pledges.

5. Check in with participants on their pledge raising and donations received.

6. Hold the pledge-raising event.

7. Follow up to collect pledges that haven't been contributed in advance of the event.

8. Evaluate and send thank yous.

As you go through the steps in detail, use the sample workplan at the end of the chapter to create a timeline and task list.

Step 1: Make a Plan

Set a date for the event to take place, making sure you can secure the location (the bowling lanes for bowling, city streets for a walk-a-thon, a pool for a swim-a-thon) and get permits if needed. Decide on your fundraising goal, which will tell you how many participants you will need. Assuming that each volunteer walker, bowler, swimmer, or runner can raise at least $500 from their contacts, you'll need to recruit ten volunteers to reach a fundraising goal of $5,000. Inevitably, people may not be able to collect all of their pledges, so you'll likely want to recruit more participants or make people's pledge goal slightly higher than the actual amount you need them to raise.

Step 2: Recruit Volunteers

The key to raising money with pledge events is getting people involved who are willing to take part in the activity *and* solicit people they know to donate in support of their efforts. You can also ask volunteers to recruit others to join the effort and to serve as team captains. In addition to expanding the number of potential donors who can be asked for support, this also provides a way to share the work of engaging, motivating, and supporting the participants in their fundraising efforts.

For a pledge-raising event, it's important to assure potential volunteers that they don't need to have to be pros in the activity to participate, have fun, and raise money. Use the Volunteer Recruitment Form in Resource A on page 187 to identify people who might be willing to help out in this and other ways. Here are the things you'll be recruiting people to do:

- Bowl, dance, walk, swim, bike, run, whatever activity you decide to do.

- Seek donations to support their participation.

- Schedule the event at the venue and get permits.

- Draft a sample letter requesting support.

- Check in with team members on how their pledge-gathering is going.

- Help out with logistics on the day of the event.

- Follow up with participants after the event to collect pledges for cash or check contributions.

- Send thank yous to volunteers and donors.

Step 3: Secure Space Rental and Permits (If Applicable)

Give your group enough lead time to find a venue appropriate for the number of people you'll be accommodating (participants in the activity and people cheering them on). Try to get the space for the pledge-raising event donated or rented at a low rate. It might be helpful to be somewhat flexible about the date of your event to take advantage of any free or low-cost spaces.

If your event requires a venue where you need to arrange for reservations or permits, you'll want to start the process at least a couple of months in advance. For example, with a bowl-a-thon, many bowling lanes are reserved by leagues, so reserving multiple lanes for your event may mean finding a less popular time or being flexible with dates. You can also ask if the venue can provide an in-kind donation. Sticking with the bowl-a-thon example, bowling alleys will often provide free shoe rentals. If the lanes won't donate the games or the shoes, you can ask the volunteers to pay for the cost of playing. When making reservations, plan on about four people per lane. Two games with four people per lane should take between an hour and a half and two hours.

Step 4: Conduct a Training or Orientation for Volunteers, and Start Asking for Donations and Pledges

Bring people together to share why they're fundraising for your group and learn about the process of soliciting pledges, how to make a compelling pitch, and what the overall goals of the pledge-raising event are. At this gathering, share pledge instructions. See Sample Instructions to Bowlers for a template.

SAMPLE INSTRUCTIONS TO BOWLERS

Thank you for agreeing to participate in the Bowl-a-thon for Health, a fundraiser for our local community health center. Your efforts will help us raise much-needed funds to start a peer counseling program for teens on sexuality and reproductive health.

Here's what we're asking you to do:

❏ Using the attached pledge form, solicit people you know to sponsor you in the upcoming bowl-a-thon. They can either make their donation right away or agree to pay their pledge once you've completed the activity. If you're planning to send an email or text requesting support and then follow up with your potential pledgers by phone, use the sample message in this packet as a guide to writing your own or just use it as is.

❏ Complete your pledge form with whatever money you've collected in advance to susana@communityhealth.org by no later than Friday, November 28. If you have cash or check donations, you can drop them off at our office.

❏ Arrive at the bowling alley at noon, ready to play! You will be matched up with three other bowlers to play with. If you already have a group that wants to bowl together, please let Susana know in advance.

❏ Follow up with your pledgers the week after the bowl-a-thon, and drop off any cash or checks you collect.

Essential Information:

Date and time of bowl-a-thon: Saturday, December 5, 2:00–5:00 P.M.

Location: Community Lanes, 2500 Main Street

Have questions or need more information? Call or email Susana Gomez, (555) 555-5555, susana@communityhealth.org.

In their orientation packet, it's helpful to include a sample email/text that volunteers can use in reaching out to their contacts to ask them for support. For example:

> *Hi, _____! It's time for the annual Walk-a-Thon for Save the Cute Kittens. As you know, Save the Cute Kittens is where I adopted my beloved Kimchi and Sprout and have volunteered for the last four years. I am trying to raise $1,000 to help them continue to rescue, foster, and get cute kittens adopted. Can you click on the link below and contribute what you can so Save the Cute Kittens can continue to make a difference? Thank you so much! I appreciate you!*

Allow three to four weeks for people to collect pledges before the event. With more time, you lose momentum; with less time, you have the obvious drawback of volunteers not reaching as many potential sponsors as possible.

We recommend online fundraising pages that volunteers create to promote and track their fundraising asks. After setting up a page, they send emails or texts to their networks with a link to their page. Many online fundraising platforms offer this feature free of charge. If online fundraising pages aren't feasible or ideal for your community, pledge forms like the one in Worksheet 10.1 will help you track contributors' names, the amounts pledged, and the total collected. For any pledge not made through online donations, ask participants to collect contributors' emails and phone numbers to thank them, share how the event went, add them to your newsletter, and make future solicitations. This is especially important if this is part of an ongoing project or organization.

For guidance on asking individuals for money, see Resource C on page 189 and Tips on Asking for Money to Sponsor Your Participation on the following page.

WORKSHEET 10.1
Sample Pledge Form

SPONSOR NAME	SPONSOR PHONE	SPONSOR EMAIL	DATE SOLICITED	TYPE OF SOLICITATION	DATE OF FOLLOW-UP	TYPE OF FOLLOW-UP	RESULT	AMOUNT PLEDGED	DATE PLEDGES COLLECTED	AMOUNT COLLECTED
Cecilia Ortiz	(323) 555-4444	cortiz@igc.org	5/25	Email	6/5	Call	Yes	$35	6/30	$35

TIPS ON ASKING FOR MONEY TO SPONSOR YOUR PARTICIPATION

Most of your follow-up calls are likely to be short and casual—that is, you'll be asking someone you know to support your efforts, and they will already have received your text or email about it. But if you want to feel more prepared and confident about picking up the phone, here are some things to think about:

❑ Relax and be yourself—you're calling people who know and like you!

❑ Remind the person why you're calling near the beginning of the conversation.

❑ Assume support, be confident, and be as direct as possible ("We're working to win . . . " or "I know this issue is something you and I both care a lot about").

❑ Use your own words. Don't read from a script.

❑ Listen; give people a chance to speak, ask a question, or voice an opinion about the issue. Don't talk *at* them; instead, aim for an interaction. You may be surprised that your prospect is already interested in what you're raising money for or wants to share their thoughts and concerns.

❑ If someone asks you a question that you don't know the answer to, be honest and tell them you don't know. Let them know you'll get back to them (and then make a note of it and *do* get back to them or make sure someone else does).

❑ Keep it short and simple. Be clear, concise, and direct.

❑ Ask for a specific amount of money.

❑ Once you make the ask, be silent. Let them think about it and answer. If you need to, slowly count to twenty in your head to keep yourself from filling the space with nervous chatter.

❑ Once they make a specific commitment, thank them and make sure they have what they need to make a contribution. If they need to think about it, ask if there are any questions you can answer right now. If they still need to think, make a specific time to call them back (and then follow up).

❑ Thank them for their time.

❑ Remember that practice makes perfect!

Step 5: Check In with Participants on Their Pledge Raising

Check-ins are key to any successful fundraising effort, and they're the organizer's main task. If you have fundraising teams, with someone leading each team (team captain), the team captain should do the follow-up. In this case, the main event organizer will be in charge of receiving and sharing updates with those team captains.

Depending on how often you're in regular contact with the volunteers, the timing will vary, but momentum must build to the day of the event. This involves both gathering updates from individual volunteers and sharing current progress and needs with all volunteers. If you have an office that volunteers or members are likely to visit regularly, consider having a sign-up poster at the office where volunteers add their names and the number of sponsors they have. If you have a website, create a page that is updated regularly with the number of sponsors solicited and the amount of money raised to date. Use recruitment calls, texts, and emails to urge people to become participants. The biggest motivator, however, is that volunteers believe in the group and want to help raise money to support it.

Step 6: Hold the Pledge-Raising Event

One or two organizers are needed for the day's event, depending on the size of the group. Confirm your reservation with the venue the week before. As participants arrive, orient them to the space and the event plan. At the end, you can give out inexpensive, funny prizes to add to the group's enjoyment and also as an excuse to bring people together, thank them for coming out, and encourage them to go collect any outstanding pledges. For example, entertaining categories for a dance-a-thon might include Most Original Form, Most Enthusiastic, and Best Dressed.

Step 7: Follow Up to Collect Pledges That Haven't Been Contributed in Advance of the Event

Keep the momentum going after the pledge-raising event by having participants go back to their donors who haven't yet fulfilled their pledges. Sponsors (donors) might also want to hear about how the event went, how many people participated, and how much money was raised, so plan to do a brief write-up and include some photos too. As soon as possible after the event, remind participants by email, text, and phone to follow up with their pledgers who have not yet contributed and encourage them to do so. Otherwise, momentum will be lost—and so will some of the money pledged.

Step 8: Evaluate and Send Thank Yous

Evaluating your event will give you important information about whether you met the goals you set for it, as well as areas for improvement for future events. Here are some questions to ask:

- Did you meet your financial goal, both gross (that is, the total income from the event) and net (what was left after expenses)?

- How many people participated in the activity itself and in donating?

- Are your key leaders who worked on this project excited to work together on other fundraising or non-fundraising projects?

- Are there things that you would change about the pledge-raising event or logistics if you did it again?

Even if you didn't meet your fundraising goals, analyzing why is just as important as if you did. The successes and mistakes you make are important lessons to pass on. Your team should also recommend whether this event should be repeated—if not, why not, and if so, how. If you decide to do a pledge-raising event again, all your records—evaluation records, donor records, workplans, invitation originals, and so on—will make it much easier for people doing an event like this another time, and will probably help them bring in more money as well. Also, your volunteers have worked hard to put on this fundraiser, so draw out all the successes and celebrate.

After pledges have been collected, ask participants to send thank yous to their supporters. If you plan to do future fundraising activities, let the contributors know that you will keep them informed of the progress of your work and will include them in your newsletter. Many who first give through a pledge event will continue to support your work from one year to the next.

Send those who participated in the event a thank you as well, acknowledging the specific amount they raised, giving the overall score or result, and telling them how much money was raised because of their efforts.

NNAF Bowl-a-Thon

For over ten years, the National Network of Abortion Funds (NNAF) hosted an annual bowl-a-thon, providing support to their member funds around the country to carry out bowl-a-thons in their communities. Like the rest of the local funds' work, the bowl-a-thons were carried out primarily by volunteers.

From the beginning, the bowl-a-thon was not just a great fundraiser but also a way to introduce energetic young leadership and new volunteers to abortion funds.

The bowl-a-thon raised $175,000 that first year (2009) and grew by leaps and bounds every year after, raising over $2 million in 2019. It has boosted the resources and visibility of abortion funds while also being seriously meaningful and tons of fun. Now it is run as a fund-a-thon, where local funds do their own annual pledge-raising activity as part of this national effort.

Nokomis Healthy Seniors Program Clean-a-Thon

Nokomis Healthy Seniors Program, based in Minneapolis, helps seniors continue to live independently in their homes. Board members organized a clean-a-thon in which they recruited volunteers to spend a Saturday morning cleaning the homes of some of the seniors the group serves. The volunteers went in teams and tackled cleaning projects that were difficult for the seniors to do themselves, such as washing windows and scrubbing floors. Before the day of the clean-a-thon, volunteers asked friends and acquaintances to sponsor them in their volunteer cleaning effort by giving a financial contribution to the organization. The first year of the clean-a-thon, with virtually no staff involvement, the volunteers raised $2,000. The second year, with a little experience under their belts, they raised more than $4,000, made possible partly by a matching gift from a local corporation.

Protest-a-Thon Against Westboro Baptist Church

A Michigan business owner employed a creative use of the pledge event to raise money for LGBTQIA causes. It was inspired as a way to put a negative spin on the doings of Fred Phelps, the infamous anti-gay pastor of the Westboro Baptist Church in Topeka, Kansas, who organized pickets around the country in the early 2000s to assert that God hated gay people. Phelps's group used outrageous tactics, such as protesting at the funerals of gay people. He hit the national spotlight when his group protested the funeral of Matthew Sheperd, the twenty-one-year-old gay man brutally killed in Wyoming in 1998.

Keith Orr, co-owner of Ann Arbor queer bar Aüt Bar, urged people to make pledges based on the length of time the Westboro protestors stayed outside his business. "We had some pledge a dollar a minute, and others pledge only a nickel a minute, but it all added up," he said. In his first action, he made $8,000 for a local gay rights organization. In Huntington, West Virginia, in a similar response to a Phelps local protest, groups or individuals pledged donations for each minute of Phelps's rally or for each time his protesters said certain words. Flat-fee pledges were also accepted. The money collected went to the local human relations commission to support diversity education.

In conjunction with the fundraiser, a local coalition of groups hosted a speak-out against Phelps, and the Huntington High School Gay-Straight Alliance (now Genders and Sexualities Alliance) scheduled a "Go-love" rally and dance.

WORKPLAN

Workplan 10.1 provides a summary of the key steps necessary to implement this fundraising strategy and an estimated time frame for each step. It is meant to be a template from which to create your own plan and your own timeline. By taking the time to create a plan and timeline, you'll be more organized, more likely to avoid last-minute crises, and ultimately more successful in raising the money you need.

WORKPLAN 10.1
Pledge-Raising Event

WHAT	WHO	1	2	3	4	5	6	7	8	9	10	DONE
1. Make a plan.		×										
2. Recruit volunteers.			×									
3. Secure space rental and permits (if applicable).			×									
4. Conduct a training or orientation for volunteers, and start asking for donations and pledges.				×								
5. Check in with participants on their pledge raising.						×	×	×	×			
6. Hold the pledge-raising event.									×			
7. Follow up to collect pledges that haven't been contributed in advance of the event.										×	×	
8. Evaluate and send thank yous.											×	

11

Silent and Virtual Auctions

There are three major kinds of auctions: live auctions with a skilled auctioneer; silent auctions, where people write their bids next to displayed items or submit bids via an online tool; and virtual auctions. This chapter will focus on silent and virtual auctions, as live auctions require an experienced and persuasive auctioneer and greater access to resources than what volunteers generally have.

Silent auctions are a great add-on to a community fundraiser, house party, or other gathering. Virtual auctions are better as a stand-alone fundraising strategy. With a virtual auction, people go to a website, view the items to bid on, and submit their bid. Anyone familiar with websites like eBay will understand the process of placing bids online.

This chapter describes how to organize both an in-person silent auction and a virtual one, either of which can raise between $500 and $5,000 (and sometimes more if there are big-ticket items).

BEST USES

Silent auctions can be a lot of fun, both for those organizing and for the people attending. As an add-on to a special event, it's possible to do a silent auction on a scale small enough to keep it manageable and still raise money. At a community potluck, for example, auctioning off ten to twenty low-budget items could add $250 to $1,000 to your event's income.

The key to a successful silent auction is the combination of donations of high-quality goods and services that people will want and a large enough group interested in bidding on them.

Virtual auctions are worth considering if you're not planning to hold an event, you have a large enough list of people to whom you can promote the activity, and you're fairly confident that they'll bid on the items you're able to get donated. Virtual auctions lend themselves to a geographically dispersed community because they don't require people to go anywhere to participate. They also have the advantage of not being time-bound to a specific date and time but can go on over the course of a week or longer.

THINGS TO CONSIDER

Remember that the donated items must be easily sent to the winners; moreover, some items won't work for people outside of your community. For example, a dinner for two in Chicago won't get many bids from your supporters in Houston.

Silent auctions are labor-intensive to organize and require a core of dedicated volunteers. Without a team approach, too much work will fall on the shoulders of too few people. There's a lot to keep track of in planning and running a silent auction, so this is a strategy for people who are extremely attentive to detail.

Both silent and virtual auctions need enough people to attend and participate in bidding. According to auctioneer Sandy Bradley, author of *Benefit Auctions: A Fresh Formula for Grassroots Fundraising*, you need critical mass for a "real-time" silent auction to succeed financially. She suggests at least twenty-five people in the bidding audience and at least two people for every item you're auctioning. In other words, an auction with fifteen items to be bid on needs at least thirty people willing to place bids.

Assuming your silent auction is happening during an event, you need to regularly remind attendees of when the silent auction is happening and how to bid. People volunteering at registration should share information about the auction, and emcees should give regular announcements between programming segments. Ideally, the auction items are placed in a high-traffic area.

For virtual auctions, you'll need to consider how you're going to get the items to the people who purchase them, so avoid soliciting auction items like furniture.

Virtual auctions aren't the best strategy if you're trying to build a sense of community, if you want to celebrate something with a group of people, or if you want to deepen people's connection to the issue you're raising money for. However, they are a way to get people who are more peripheral to your group to donate money to the group for something they want that also supports a good cause.

COSTS

When producing a silent auction, consider the following items as potential costs and try to get as many as possible donated (many of these items would also be necessary for an event at which the auction is an add-on activity):

- Space
- Tables and chairs
- Materials for displaying auction items

If the auction is virtual:

- Virtual auction platform fees

Whether the auction is silent or virtual:

- Invitation design
- Publicity (Resource G on page 194 covers ways to publicize your auction)
- Catalog design

As you go through the steps in detail, use the sample workplan at the end of the chapter to create a timeline and task list.

STEPS TO TAKE

1. Make a plan.
2. Recruit volunteers.
3. Prepare volunteers to solicit items.

4. Solicit items to be auctioned.

5. Plan the program and logistics of the auction.

6. Publicize the auction.

7. Make follow-up calls and texts and track progress.

8. Make final preparations.

9. Hold the auction.

10. Send thank yous and evaluate.

Step 1: Make a Plan

You'll need to decide on a fundraising goal and date for the auction and create a timeline detailing what has to be done. For a virtual auction, you want it to be open over the course of multiple days. Once you know how much money you want to raise, plan to obtain donations of goods and services worth twice that amount. This way, you'll be able to meet your goal even if bids amount to only 50 percent of the value of each item. For example, if you want the auction to raise $5,000, you'll need to have items worth a total of $10,000 to be auctioned. Moreover, because about half the people you ask to donate items will decline, you'll need to plan to solicit $20,000 worth of items.

Step 2: Recruit Volunteers

Use Resource A, the Volunteer Recruitment Form, to identify people you can recruit to help out with the auction. Here are some of the things you'll want to ask people to do:

- Solicit items to be auctioned.

- Organize the logistics of the event.

- Help publicize the event.

- Compile lists of people and organizations to send publicity to about the auction.

- Follow up on invitations sent to increase turnout to the auction.

- Help out with the auction itself.

Step 3: Prepare Volunteers to Solicit Items

Before sending volunteers out to solicit items for the auction, bring them together to brainstorm who to ask and to orient them to the process of asking. You'll want to come up with a list of who is being solicited to avoid having one person inadvertently asked by two different solicitors.

It's helpful if the auction items are grouped by category, such as vacations, services, household goods, or restaurants. Make a list of all the vendors who might donate something and what you want to ask them for, such as dinner for two, a weekend getaway at a vacation cabin, and so on. If the auction is virtual, consider items that are easy and affordable to mail or drop off to the winning bidders. Gift cards are much more convenient to mail or send a link to than a kitchen appliance.

Remember that people who own small businesses, particularly storefronts, get asked for donations frequently. They might turn you down for a number of reasons not having to do with your group—they may have policies against making donations, they may have donated to five other causes and are not giving to any more at the moment, or it may be a hard time for their business. Resource F lists some ideas for items to solicit.

Step 4: Solicit Items to Be Auctioned

In this step, volunteers solicit the items for the auction. In cases where the volunteer knows the prospect, they can just call and follow up with a confirmation letter if the person agrees to donate something. In other cases, they might want to send a short email or visit to their business first, stating what they'd like the person to donate and what cause or organization the auction is supporting.

Give this step plenty of time—two months is ideal. People need that time to make calls and visits to ask for donations, track prospects down to get their commitments to donate items, and then actually obtain the items.

Solicitors can help merchants think about how giving an item to your organization is good for their business. Selling points to the merchant include the number of people expected to attend the auction who will see the merchant's name listed with the item, other publicity you're going to do, a promise not to ask for another item this year, or whatever is true for your group. You will likely have greater success getting items donated by merchants that you know personally, that your organization does business with, or that believe in the cause you're raising money for. Start with them. See the sample email asking for a donation to your auction on the following page.

Dear Friend (or Merchant),

I'm writing to ask you to help support a newly formed artists cooperative, Art for All (A4A). This nonprofit group highlights the work of artists with disabilities in our community. We're planning the first of what we hope will be an annual event: a community potluck and silent auction. I'm hoping you will donate a gift certificate of $25 (or more) to your store to be auctioned off at this event.

The purpose of A4A is to break the isolation that many people with disabilities experience in our community by bringing disabled artists together in exhibitions and in creating communal art projects. We are an all-volunteer project and need to raise money to pay for the expenses of producing exhibits and other programs. This year, our goal is $10,000. Your support of the upcoming silent auction will help us to reach that goal.

We expect about one hundred people to attend the auction, and more than one thousand others will hear about the event and about your business supporting our work through our website and upcoming newsletter.

Let us know if you can contribute a gift card (or other item) to this fundraising effort. We greatly appreciate whatever you can give.

Here's a form to fill out with your pledge [link to online form]. And of course, let me know if you have any questions about it.

Thank you so much for considering this request.

Sincerely,

(Name of volunteer)

Include a form like the Auction Donor Form with your email to help you keep track of what's being donated and get any instructions about how the gift should be handled.

During the time that volunteers are soliciting donated items, check in with them regularly to see how they're doing and what kind of support they need if they're having a hard time completing their solicitations. Be prepared to help people with problem-solving and to provide encouragement to keep the momentum going.

Worksheet 11.1 (on page 140) can help you track progress getting auction items.

AUCTION DONOR FORM

Thank you for your contribution to A4A's silent auction, taking place on June 25. Please complete this form no later than May 18.

DONATION: Please describe each donation in detail for display and catalog purposes—for example, "Two $50 gift cards," "A one-hour Swedish massage," "Frequent flyer miles for one ticket anywhere in the United States." If possible, please include a photograph or information sheet. Be sure to specify the location, if applicable, and any limitations, such as availability or excluded items.

_____

_____

- ☐ Items or gift card are included.
- ☐ Please make up a gift card for me.
- ☐ I will send or deliver my donation by May 18.
- ☐ Please send a volunteer to pick up my donation.

Offer expiration date: _____

Retail value: $_____

Minimum bid: _____

- ☐ IMPORTANT! The donor will be acknowledged in auction displays and catalog. To remain anonymous, please check here.

_____ Business donor _____ Individual donor

Donor Name _____

Contact Name (if business donor) _____

Mailing Address _____

City, State, ZIP _____

Email _____

Phone Number _____

Donor Signature _____

Date _____

Please fill out and submit this form by May 18.

WORKSHEET 11.1
Sample Auction Items Tracking Form

NAME	ITEM TYPE	PHONE NUMBER	EMAIL	DATE EMAIL SENT	DATE OF FOLLOW-UP (CALL OR IN PERSON)	RESULTS	NEXT STEPS
Rosie's Restaurant	Dinner for two	(555) 555-5555	info@rosiesrestaurant.com	5/20	6/1	Yes to gift certificate for $50	Rosie will submit form and drop off gift certificate.
Gerry's Gems	Gift certificate	(444) 444-4444	hello@gerrysgems.com	5/25	6/8	Can't this year	Said OK to try again next year.

Step 5: Plan the Program and Logistics of the Auction

Once the process of soliciting items for the auction is underway, you can start paying more attention to the details required to hold a successful event. If you're holding it in person, there are many logistical decisions to make. First, consider whether people will sit or stand during different parts of the event, and figure that into your site selection. Second, find a venue for the auction that is large enough to accommodate the number of people you expect for the program you envision and has enough well-lit space to display all of the auction items. In addition, you'll need a place to store the donated items ahead of time. If the auction is a stand-alone event, you'll want to consider food and drink to offer attendees.

For virtual auctions, your first focus will be on selecting the virtual auction platform. You can find virtual auction platforms from an internet search. Some platforms are free or offer free features, though most have costs associated with their usage. You can also talk to others who have used various auction platforms about what they've liked or found easiest to use for those within your price range. Common pricing models for these platforms are as follows:

FLAT FEE Charging a flat fee per virtual auction or year (generally hundreds of dollars)

COMMISSION-BASED Charging a commission based on the total amount raised during the virtual auction (usually 5 to 10 percent with a fee of $0 to $50 per event)

PER ITEM Charging a fee per item listed in the virtual auction (this is less common but can be suitable for smaller events, generally less than $1 per item with a minimum of $10 to $20 per event)

Once you've decided on the platform you'll use, you're ready to post the items to be auctioned off. Take photographs of any physical items that will be auctioned to upload on item postings. For tickets, gift certificates, and so on, create a generic image to use. Decide on a minimum bid for each item and the increments for increasing a bid.

Step 6: Publicize the Auction

This step has three parts:

SEND INVITATIONS BY EMAIL. Create an invitation that makes it easy for people to respond and send in a contribution even if they can't participate in the auction. In addition, you may want to create a flyer that you can send to organizations for posting and that they can distribute to other people. In addition to sending the invitation and/or flyers to everyone on your list, ask volunteers to send them out to their contacts as well. If you already have some auction items donated, including a list of sample items that will be auctioned off may entice people to come. If you have a lot of lead time, you can even put together a catalog with pictures or at least descriptions of the majority of the auction items.

USE YOUR WEBSITE AND SOCIAL MEDIA. If your organization has a website and a social media presence, post information and the flyer about the auction there, with examples of items that are being auctioned and all the details visitors need to attend. Include an RSVP link.

USE WHATEVER OTHER FREE PUBLICITY OUTLETS YOU CAN THINK OF. Resource G on page 194 covers some no- to low-cost ideas to help you spread the word.

You will want to generate as much interest as possible in the virtual auction using email and social media, especially in the final days.

Step 7: Make Follow-Up Calls and Texts and Track Progress

The success of a silent auction—that is, how much money you raise—depends on how many people attend the event and engage in the bidding. Ask your volunteers to follow up on the invitations they sent by calling the invitees about two weeks before the auction is scheduled to take place. A reminder call like this can make the difference between someone attending the event—or, in the case of a virtual auction, bidding for items—or not. Consider getting your volunteers together for two evenings during which everyone calls their lists and anyone else who received an invitation.

As the auction nears, have regular check-ins with volunteers to go over the number of invites and confirmed RSVPs. Use a shared tracking sheet like the one in Worksheet 11.2 so you each know who is inviting whom and have an up-to-date count of RSVPs.

WORKSHEET 11.2
Sample Event Invitation and Turnout Tracking

NAME	PHONE	EMAIL	ADDRESS	DATE INVITATION SENT	DATE OF CONFIRMATION CALL/TEXT	ATTENDING?	NOTES
Ernest Hum	(601) 222-5353	ernestm@email.com	15 Fifth Ave.	7/17	7/28	No	
Joan Swan	(601) 222-1234	joan@email.com	316 Aspen	7/17	8/1	Yes	Janice's sister

Step 8: Make Final Preparations

For silent auctions, the details of organizing the event include setting up the space to allow for the best presentation of items and traffic flow so people can easily place bids.

Prepare a form to place in front of each item that describes the item, lists the donor name (if not anonymous), and indicates the minimum bid and in what increments additional bids can be placed. For example, a gift basket of skin care products that would sell at your local bath store for $30 might have a minimum bid of $20, with increments of $5. A trip to Santa Fe, flight and accommodations included, worth $2,000, might have a minimum bid of $1,000, with bidding increments of $100. See Sample Bid Sheet for Silent Auction to get started.

SAMPLE BID SHEET FOR SILENT AUCTION

Item 15 (This corresponds to the number in the catalog.)

Item: One-hour Swedish massage by Sophia Walker

Value: $75

Minimum bid: $50

Minimum additional bid: $5

NAME OF BIDDER	AMOUNT OF BID	PHONE	EMAIL
	$		
	$		
	$		
	$		
	$		

Finally, assign volunteers to the various activities that need to be carried out during the auction, as detailed in Volunteer Duties for Silent Auction.

VOLUNTEER DUTIES FOR SILENT AUCTION

While this may seem like a lot of tasks requiring a large number of volunteers, each role can be handled by one person in most cases.

Check-in Table Attendants

Hand out programs or catalogs.

Greeters

These volunteers greet the arrivals and answer questions, such as where to find restrooms and refreshments, and how the bidding works. They can also serve as floaters between tables and other volunteer stations to help out wherever needed, including answering questions about items up for bid.

Recorder

This volunteer keeps track of winning bids and each winner's contact information. At the end of the auction, they bring the bidding forms to the cashier, who collects payment from the winning bidders. These receipts record the auction item and item number listed in the catalog, the winner's name, and the amount the item sold for.

Checkout Attendants

Several people should be assigned to this job. Depending on how many people attend the auction, you may want to break up the checkout and cashier lines into sections (for example, bidder last names starting with A through G in one line, H through M in another, and so on). The cashier station should organize the winning bids in alphabetical order so that when the winning bidder comes to pay and pick up their item, it can be found quickly. Most of the goods should be in the cashier area so the cashier or a helper can turn over the goods at this point. Items too large to carry may require special delivery or pickup arrangements.

Keep in mind that the people who have donated items to the auction may follow the progress of the bids closely. While the bidder wants to buy an item for less than it costs, the donor won't be pleased to see the item sold for a fraction of its value. This is especially true for things that don't have a fixed value, such as art or handmade crafts. For example, one organization auctioned a hand-knitted sweater worth $150 for $25, hurting the donor's feelings and causing a rift with the volunteer who had solicited the item. For this reason, set minimum bids at a level that will ensure the items are sold for an amount the donor will find reasonable.

For a virtual auction, ensure that you have a volunteer available to respond to questions that participants may have with no more than two hours turnaround time during the most common bidding times, like 9 A.M. to 9 P.M. This would involve logging into the auction platform and monitoring any emails that have come in from bidders. Consider assigning one volunteer for each of three shifts (e.g., 9 A.M. to 1 P.M., 1 P.M. to 5 P.M., and 5 P.M. to 9 P.M.).

Step 9: Hold the Auction

It's a good idea to create and distribute the auction rules to everyone as they arrive at the auction. See the Auction Rules sidebar for a sample you can use.

In addition, to ensure that people start bidding, line up a few volunteers to bid on items early on to create momentum. Few people like to be the first ones bidding on something unless it's a very popular item.

AUCTION RULES

❏ All sales are final. No refunds or returns allowed.

❏ All items are sold "as is" and must be removed at the end of the event. Payments may be made by credit card, check, or cash.

❏ A paid "receipt" is required to remove an item.

❏ The organization reserves the right to withdraw any item prior to the call for bids.

❏ A minimum bid has been established on all items.

It's important that the people attending are serious about bidding. Otherwise, you risk both not selling enough to raise the money you had planned for and not having the excitement of bidding to make the event enjoyable for the guests. One option is to bundle smaller items into a bigger package. Another way to ensure enthusiasm is to assess the donated items to make sure they'll be of interest to bidders. If you feel something is worth much more than people attending the auction will be willing to spend on it, arrange to sell it outside of the auction. For example, at a neighborhood association's auction to which residents donated many wonderful items, an antique brooch was donated that the auction organizers had appraised by an antiques dealer. While the brooch was certainly worth its $250 appraised value, it was too old-fashioned for the audience's taste. To make full use of the donated item, the organization sold it to an antique jewelry dealer for more money than they thought it would bring at the auction.

As the auction gets underway, monitor the level of bidding activity to determine if you need to increase publicity to get more people involved. Once the auction is closed, make sure winners have paid for their items before they receive them.

As part of preparation for the auction, think through how people will pay for and collect the items they've acquired. You want to avoid having a pile-up of winners coming to pay for their items at the end of the evening, which makes an otherwise enjoyable experience irritating. Have several volunteers ready to collect money and distribute the items, as well as enough space set aside for that task. If at all possible, arrange to accept credit card payments and checks for the items people have bought. This option is especially important if you have any high-ticket items, such as expensive artwork or vacations. As the winning bidders pay for their treasures, remind them that these donations are not tax-deductible.

Step 10: Send Thank Yous and Evaluate

Send thank yous to everyone who attended the auction, sold tickets, and donated items.

If you think you might want to conduct another auction in the future, evaluation is crucial to making improvements and potentially raising more money the next time. Your evaluation can be a simple set of notes jotted down soon after the auction is over, perhaps at a final wrap-up meeting of the auction team. Note how many items were sold, which were the most popular, and any problems with the volunteers, merchants, or logistics. Create documents with all the information about the auction, including lists of who donated items, who purchased items, and who volunteered, and notes about timing and other issues. The following year, it will be much simpler to organize the auction if a committee can pull out the documents and benefit from the previous year's experience.

The Box Show™

Gallery Route One, a nonprofit art organization with an artist-/member-run gallery in a rural community in Northern California, hosts a silent auction every year to raise money for their community programs. The Box Show™ features inventive and ingenious works of art created from a simple pine box that each contributing artist is given. Their boxes are displayed in the gallery throughout the month of August, during which time visitors to the gallery—or on their virtual auction platform—can bid on them. The auction is the gallery's biggest fundraiser of the year and is run almost entirely by volunteers. The first show was in 1998, and it now auctions 150 unique artworks every year. The popularity of the event is evident from both the wait list of artists who want to participate and the $20,000 plus that is raised each year from the sales of the boxes.

La ColectiVA

La ColectiVA is a social justice collective of Latinx activists in Northern Virginia whose work focuses primarily on immigrant rights issues. The group's LiberArte event raises money for legal fees for individuals in immigration detention facing deportation. The event is free to attend and money is raised from a silent auction that features art made and donated by local artists. In their most successful auction, fifty people attended, and the group raised about $3,000. In addition to fundraising, the event has served to build community and provide popular education.

WORKPLAN

Workplan 11.1 on the following page summarizes the key steps necessary to implement this fundraising strategy and an estimated time frame for each step. It is meant to be a template from which to create your own plan and your own timeline. By taking the time to create a plan and timeline, you'll be more organized, more likely to avoid last-minute crises, and ultimately more successful in raising the money you need.

WORKPLAN 11.1
Silent or Virtual Auction

WHAT	WHO	1	2	3	4	5	6	7	8	9	10	11	DONE
1. Make a plan.													
Make a budget.		×											
Decide on a silent or virtual auction.		×											
Identify potential volunteer roles.		×											
2. Recruit volunteers.			×	×									
3. Prepare volunteers to solicit items.				×	×								
4. Solicit items to be auctioned.													
Solicit items.				×	×	×	×	×	×				
Make follow-up calls to volunteer solicitors.					×	×	×	×	×				
5. Plan the program and logistics of the auction.			×	×									
6. Publicize the auction.													
Design and send invitations.					×	×	×						
Prepare other publicity (neighborhood forums, flyers, local paper, etc.).							×	×					
7. Make follow-up calls and texts and track progress.									×	×			
8. Make final preparations.													
Prepare auction catalog.								×	×	×			
Set up for auction.										×	×		
Finalize the details on volunteers to help out.											×		
9. Hold the auction.											×		
10. Evaluate and send thank yous.												×	

12

Raffles

common, easy, and fun way to raise almost any amount of money—although generally on the lower end than what's possible with other strategies—is a raffle. Almost everyone is familiar with raffles, having bought tickets for them and perhaps even won a prize in one. Because raffles are such a commonly used fundraising technique, most people don't realize that organizing one involves a lot of details that you'll need to stay on top of. However, raffles are simple to carry out and can be a lot of fun.

Raffles appeal to people's desire to win something and support a good cause with a very small donation at the same time. Because raffles make $1 to $10 a legitimate gift, people with little money can feel they've given the right amount, and people who don't care that much about your organization but don't want to disappoint you can contribute easily.

The way raffles work is that your group gets items donated for the prizes that winners will receive. These may include but aren't limited to cash, services such as massages or window washing, trips, and gift cards. Generally, there are five to ten prizes, one of which is a grand prize. Grand prizes can be anything from a free weekend at a vacation home or bed and breakfast to an airline ticket for domestic travel to a dinner for two at a fancy restaurant. Tickets are sold for between $1 and $10 each, and buyers are incentivized to buy multiple tickets with offers like "$5 per ticket or 10 tickets for $35." Many more tickets are sold than prizes available, so there's suspense and luck involved. At an appointed day and time, the winning tickets are drawn. This can be done "live" (that is, in person with tickets drawn from a large container) or virtually, using an online raffle platform. Aside from the tickets sold, there is no other source of income in a raffle. The costs can be kept low.

BEST USES

Raffles are a good option under the following circumstances:

- To bring in additional income as part of an event (you can sell raffle tickets at check-in and have dedicated volunteers walk through the event to sell tickets to attendees)

- When you're trying to raise money from people who are unlikely to give more than a small gift

- When the people you're trying to recruit to help raise money are shy about asking for money directly but less intimidated by the prospect of selling an inexpensive raffle ticket

- When you don't need to raise an enormous amount of money

- When you have a lot of people willing to sell tickets

THINGS TO CONSIDER

Raffles have to be organized carefully so that they don't violate gambling laws. Although laws prohibiting gambling are rarely enforced with raffles, it's important to organize your raffle so that you're operating within legal bounds. In addition to federal and state laws, find out the laws in your community. In California, for example, you're not allowed to use the word *raffle* at all; the acceptable terminology is *opportunity drawing*.

The stickiest legal obstacle is that raffle tickets can't actually be sold. When we speak of "selling" tickets, what we should actually say is that the ticket is free and a donation of $5 (or whatever the amount determined) is requested. Technically, someone must be able to ask for and receive a ticket without giving you any money. Turning down that request would be against the law. In this chapter, we refer to "selling" the tickets because that's the common shorthand; however, keep in mind that you aren't truly selling anything.

Another risk with raffles is that, because people are handling small amounts of money, often cash, it's easy for ticket sellers to lose track of how many tickets they've sold and how much cash they've collected. See Step 7 for ideas on how to minimize the number of tickets and amount of cash that disappear, but also assume that you'll never get a 100 percent return on the tickets you distribute to volunteers.

COSTS

- Printing of raffle tickets (if the raffle is in person)
- Postage for sending out prizes
- Virtual raffle platform (optional)

STEPS TO TAKE

1. Make a plan.
2. Recruit volunteers.
3. Solicit prizes.
4. Prepare tickets.
5. Distribute tickets to volunteers.
6. Motivate volunteers to keep selling.
7. Collect tickets and money.
8. Hold the drawing.
9. Send out prizes, thank yous, and evaluate.

As you go through the steps in detail, use the sample workplan at the end of the chapter to create a timeline and task list.

Step 1: Make a Plan

First, set your fundraising goal. If you have decided to sell your raffle tickets for $5 each, to raise $1,000 you'll need to sell at least two hundred tickets. Assume, too, that a volunteer can sell about twenty-five tickets over the course of the raffle. Use that formula as a way to estimate how many people you need to recruit to sell tickets. To sell two hundred tickets, then, you need eight people selling.

Also think about where the drawing will take place. Will it be part of a larger event or party, or will you do a virtual drawing using an online platform? If the latter, you'll want to do an internet search to select which online platform you want to use. You can also ask people you know who have done virtual raffle drawings which platforms they've used to help narrow down your choices and pick one that is recommended by someone you trust.

Some platforms are free or offer free features, though most have costs associated with their usage. Common pricing models for these platforms are as follows:

FLAT FEE   Charging a flat fee per raffle or year (generally $10 to $50 per month)

COMMISSION-BASED   Charging a commission based on the total amount raised during the raffle (usually 5 to 10 percent, with a fee of $0 to $50 per raffle)

PER TICKET   Charging a fee per ticket sold (this is less common but can be suitable for smaller events, generally less than $1 per ticket sold plus a transaction fee)

You can still hold an online gathering to talk up the cause and draw the winning tickets in real time. Making the drawing part of a larger event allows you to sell more tickets at the event itself.

Step 2: Recruit Volunteers

In addition to selling tickets, which is the task you most want to recruit volunteers to do, there are some other tasks you might want to ask people to help carry out:

- Draft the solicitation pitch for prizes.

- Brainstorm potential prize donors.

- Solicit prizes.

- Design and print tickets.

- Recruit ticket sellers.

- Coach and train ticket sellers.

- Organize the drawing.

- Thank everyone who helped out.

Use the Volunteer Recruitment Form in Resource A on page 187 to develop a list of potential volunteers and what you'll ask them to do.

In thinking about possible ticket sellers, consider people who work in large office buildings or unions, or who have large families or a large circle of friends. Raffles are a good opportunity to get peripheral people involved, so don't just go to your reliable volunteers who already do everything else. Ask each person if they know someone who would be good at selling tickets. People's spouses or partners, neighbors, and business partners can be recruited for this effort. You want to have as many ticket sellers as you can possibly find, both to distribute as many tickets as possible and also because some people who sign up to sell tickets will end up not doing so. Offer a fun but inexpensive prize for the person who brings in the most money selling tickets. (You may also want to award other small prizes to ticket sellers as a way to encourage sales, as described in Step 8.)

Step 3: Solicit Prizes

It's helpful if the prizes have a theme, such as vacations, services, household items, or restaurants. Make a list of all the vendors who might donate a prize, and list specifically what you want from them, such as dinner for two or a weekend cabin. Remember that people who own small businesses, particularly those in storefronts, frequently get asked to donate raffle prizes. They may have policies against doing it; they may have donated to five other worthy causes and are not taking on any more; they may be having a hard time in their business and not be able to give you anything. For those reasons, you should have at least four times as many potential sources of prizes as prizes needed.

Assign volunteers to solicit the prizes. In some cases, with people they know, a volunteer can just make a phone call and follow up with an email if the prospect agrees to donate something. In other cases, they might want to send a short outreach email first, stating what they'd like the person to donate and what cause or organization the raffle is supporting. Stress to each merchant how many people will see the tickets, how much other publicity you're going to do, that you won't ask for another item this year, or whatever is true for you. Merchants must consider how giving your organization an item will benefit their business, and you must help them with that thinking. You will have greater success getting prizes from merchants that you know personally, that your organization does business with, or that believe in the cause you're raising money for. Start with them.

The following sample appeal soliciting raffle prizes will give volunteers an example of what to write to potential donors:

> *Dear Friend (or Merchant),*
>
> *I'm writing as a volunteer with Healthy Farmers, Healthy Communities (HFHC) to ask you to help us with our project to bring a weekly farmer's market to our neighborhood. We envision the market taking place in the abandoned lot on the corner of Fifth and Grove Streets, and we are looking to raise $5,000 to clean up the lot and publicize the market to the community. We have commitments from several local farmers who are interested in selling their produce at a Saturday market, and we think there will be a lot of interest from the community.*
>
> *One of the ways we are raising money is through a raffle. We hope you would be willing to donate an item or service to this project.*
>
> *We believe that having a local place to purchase good, fresh produce will bring more customers into town, which will also benefit small businesses like yours. As you know, many residents of our community end up shopping in the malls outside of town. A weekly farmer's market will benefit all of us: local farmers, small businesses, and the people who live here.*
>
> *If you can contribute something to this fundraising effort, please fill out the linked donation form. We greatly appreciate whatever you can give.*
>
> *I will be stopping by to follow up on this email within the next week and to answer any questions you may have.*
>
> *Sincerely,*
>
> *(Name and position)*

See Resource F on page 193 for help identifying potential prize donors.

Using the Sample Donation Form as a guide, volunteers can include in their email a donor form that prospects can fill out to indicate what they're contributing.

SAMPLE DONATION FORM

HEALTHY FARMS, HEALTHY COMMUNITIES
RAFFLE DONATION FORM

Thank you for your contribution of a prize to HFHC's upcoming raffle. Please complete this form no later than March 1.

DONATION: Please describe your donation for listing on the raffle ticket—for example, "Dinner for two at Chez Moi," or "$100 gift card to Sally's Spa." Please indicate if there are any restrictions on the prize, such as limited time availability or other special instructions.

_____

_____

☐ Items or gift certificates are included.

☐ Please make up a gift certificate for me.

☐ I will send or deliver my donation by March 1.

☐ Please send a volunteer to pick up my donation.

Offer expiration date: _____

Retail value: $_____   _____

☐ IMPORTANT! The donor name will be acknowledged in publicity about the raffle. To remain anonymous, please check here.

_____ Business donor _____ Individual donor

Donor Name _____

Contact Name (if business donor) _____

Mailing Address _____

City, State, ZIP _____

Email _____

Phone Number _____

Donor Signature _____

Date _____

Please complete the form by March 1.

The Raffle Prize Tracking Form in Worksheet 12.1 will help volunteers keep track of who they've asked and what prizes have been committed.

Step 4: Prepare Tickets

In this step, your first decision will be whether to design and print physical tickets or use a virtual raffle platform for tickets:

USING VIRTUAL TICKETS For a virtual raffle, you'll use an online raffle platform that can provide the technology you need to both sell tickets and carry out a fair drawing. Volunteers then use a unique link for people to purchase tickets online or a phone app for them to purchase tickets in person.

DESIGNING AND PRINTING PHYSICAL TICKETS For physical tickets, you'll need to add a step of designing and printing them. Most print shops have predesigned ticket templates you can use, adding your own specific copy to them. Once you have the prizes, decide which will be the grand prize, the second prize, and so on, so you can feature the top prizes in the ticket design. Designing the tickets requires attention to a number of details. Refer to Sample Raffle Ticket for what should go on the tickets.

WORKSHEET 12.1
Sample Raffle Prize Tracking Form

NAME	EMAIL	PRIZE TYPE	SOLICITATION: WHO	SOLICITATION: HOW	RESULT	NEXT STEPS	NEXT OUTREACH DATE
Eli's Electronics	hello@eliselectronics.com	Gift certificate	Rashid	Send email and visit		Go to store and talk to Eli	1/25
Coco's Cafe	info@cocoscafe.com	Dinner for two	Johanna	Visit	Store owner Miriam said maybe	Call Miriam	1/22

SAMPLE RAFFLE TICKET

HEALTHY COMMUNITIES ANNUAL RAFFLE

Suggested Donation: $5.00 per ticket or 10 tickets for $35

Grand Prize: Two-night stay at a bed and breakfast in [nearby vacation destination]

Second Prize: Dinner for two at [local restaurant]

Third Prize: A weekly Community Supported Agriculture food box for three months

A benefit for Healthy Communities

DRAWING: December 10, 2025

You need not be present to win. Free ticket available on request.

Winners will be notified by email. For a list of winners, email Healthy Communities, info@healthycommunities.org.

No. 4467

Name _____

Email _____

Please send me more information on Healthy Communities.

Seller's name _____

Some phrases must be printed on the ticket, and others are simply a good idea to have there. The first two in the following list are required:

- How to get a free ticket. (This can be in small type.)

- How to see the list of winners. (This helps ensure that the prizes are actually awarded.)

- Whether the donor must be present to win. (Not requiring their attendance will help increase sales.)

- A ticket number. (This will make it easier to keep track of the tickets you have handed out to volunteers to sell. Although it may cost more to have numbers printed on the tickets, it's worth it.)

It is also critical that the ticket stub be perforated so it can be easily separated from the body of the ticket. This is another worthwhile expense. Don't try to save money by printing cheap raffle tickets. Your volunteers will not distribute them as easily, and donors will be reluctant to give their money when the ticket appears defective.

Because of the need for numbering and perforation, not all printers can print raffle tickets. Find a printer who can. Seek to have the printing donated, but don't scrimp on print costs. Notice on the sample ticket that the seller is asked to sign their name on the ticket stub. This gives you a way to identify how many tickets each volunteer sold, which could be helpful information if you decide to do a raffle again or if you're looking for enthusiastic fundraising volunteers. It also gives you a way to keep track of ticket sales for the incentive prize to the person who sold the most tickets.

To keep track of who buys tickets so you can contact them if they win a prize and go back to them later to ask for their support again, instruct the ticket sellers to make sure that email addresses (and phone numbers, if possible) are on the ticket stubs they turn in.

To promote the group holding the raffle, include a box the purchaser can check to get more information about the group's work. If you do make such an offer, be sure you go through all the tickets, pull out those with checked boxes, and add them to your newsletter list in a timely manner.

To determine how many tickets to print, add up how many tickets your volunteer workers are willing to take and compare that with your goal for the raffle, then make appropriate adjustments as needed. Print at least 10 percent more tickets than you need to reach your financial goal, as some tickets are bound to get lost or damaged.

Step 5: Distribute Tickets to Volunteers

Make a list of everyone selling tickets and the number ranges of the tickets they take. Then, using a form such as Worksheet 12.2, keep track of the ticket stubs as they are returned.

Update this tracking form at least weekly so your team can have the latest numbers of how many tickets have been sold.

Ticket sales should go on for at least one month, and can continue for two to three months. After two or three months, you'll lose momentum, and you may also have a harder time collecting the money (using cash or electronic payment apps).

WORKSHEET 12.2
Sample Raffle Ticket Sales Tracking Form

NAME	NUMBER OF TICKETS TAKEN	CHECK-IN CALLS/EMAILS			UNSOLD TICKETS RETURNED	FUNDS TURNED IN
		DATE	NUMBER OF TICKETS SOLD	FUNDS COLLECTED		
Young Min	100	5/8	20	$40		
		5/22	54	$75		
		6/10	12	$60	14	$175
TOTAL			86	$175		

For virtual raffles, volunteers can sell tickets through:

ONLINE SALES Sharing a unique link to the online platform for supporters to purchase tickets

IN-PERSON SALES Using a cell phone or tablet to sell tickets using the app's ticket feature

Step 6: Motivate Volunteers to Keep Selling

Call your volunteers at least once a week to see how they're doing with their ticket sales. Remind them of the deadline and ask that they send in stubs and cash as these accumulate. If they aren't selling as many tickets as they expected to, ask them what kind of support they need. Let them know how all the other ticket sellers are doing to encourage them to keep going. Tell them who's winning the "most sold" prize so far.

One member of the team, the raffle coordinator, should be responsible for making sure people have enough tickets to sell and that they are selling them. Raffles fail when there are not enough people selling tickets or when the people who take tickets don't sell them. Celebrate those who are doing their job and encourage those who aren't.

Every volunteer ought to sell at least twenty-five individual tickets. Most people who live in a relatively populated area can sell fifty tickets in two or three weeks with no difficulty. Some people will be able to sell one hundred tickets or more in one or two months.

Step 7: Collect Tickets and Money

Most groups find that the most difficult task in a raffle is not in getting the prizes or the volunteers, but in getting the tickets and cash back from those selling them.

Some volunteers will be careless with their ticket stubs, or they'll return stubs and promise cash later, or they may claim to have sold tickets when they really haven't. If you've encouraged people to turn in money and stubs as they go along, you'll have less difficulty than if you wait to collect all the stubs and proceeds until just before the drawing. Final submission of stubs and cash—and unsold tickets—should be due at least three days, and preferably five days, before the drawing. That way, you can ensure that you have all the tickets accounted for well ahead of time.

Step 8: Hold the Drawing

For virtual tickets, your online platform will include the functionality to take care of the drawing for you. You can assign one or two volunteers to learn that process.

For printed tickets, the drawing is held on the date printed on the ticket, either as part of another event such as a dance or auction, or in a ceremony of its own (either in person or virtually). For an in-person drawing, it's fine to have a small party for all those who worked on the raffle and sold tickets and do the drawing there. If you have good food and drink, the drawing becomes a celebration and a reward for a job well done, as well as a way to ensure that all the sold tickets are turned in on time.

Get a big box or barrel for the ticket stubs. Mix and remix the stubs thoroughly after each prize is drawn. Start with the last prize and work up to the grand prize.

After the winning ticket stubs are drawn, announce the prizes for top ticket sellers and award these. Many groups give several prizes to their ticket sellers. In addition to the person who sold the most tickets, they award a prize to the person who got the most prizes donated, the person who recruited the most other people to sell tickets, the person who sold the most tickets in a week, and the person who sold the most to a single person. Having a lot of prizes for ticket sellers is a good motivator for those who are competitive during the selling process and a nice reward at the end.

Step 9: Send Out Prizes, Thank Yous, and Evaluate

Arrange for the winners to get their prizes, either by picking them up at a designated location or receiving them in the mail.

Send a thank you to each person who sold tickets and to all the merchants and others who donated prizes.

Note how many tickets were sold out of the total number your volunteers agreed to sell, any challenges you or your volunteers had with reaching your goal, and lessons learned in trying to secure raffle prizes. Create a folder with all the information about the raffle, including lists of winners, donors, and volunteers, and any notes about timing and other issues. If you decide to do another raffle in the future, it will be much simpler if a committee can open the file and benefit from your prior experience.

Neighbors in Ministry

Neighbors in Ministry is an organization in Brevard, North Carolina, that runs an after-school program called Rise and Shine Freedom School. Some years ago, they raised $500 for the program in just two weeks through a "Back to School Shopping Spree" raffle. They printed a total of one thousand tickets and sold them for $1 each. There was only one prize—a cash gift of $500—which made the tickets easy to sell. A total of forty parents and ten board members each sold twenty tickets, bringing in $1,000, which was split evenly with the winner.

WORKPLAN

Workplan 12.1 on the following page summarizes the key steps necessary to implement this fundraising strategy and an estimated time frame for each step. It is meant to be a template from which to create your own plan and your own timeline. By taking the time to create a plan and timeline, you'll be more organized, more likely to avoid last-minute crises, and ultimately more successful in raising the money you need.

WORKPLAN 12.1
Raffles

WHAT	WHO	WHEN (WEEK NUMBER)											DONE
		1	2	3	4	5	6	7	8	9	10	11	
1. Make a plan.		×											
2. Recruit volunteers.		×											
Prepare materials.			×										
Train volunteers.				×									
Come up with ideas for raffle prizes.													
Draft forms and sample outreach.				×									
3. Solicit prizes.					×	×	×						
Make follow-up calls to volunteer solicitors.					×	×	×						
4. Prepare tickets.						×	×						
5. Distribute tickets to volunteers.							×	×	×	×	×		
6. Follow up with ticket sellers.								×	×	×	×		
7. Collect money and ticket stubs.								×	×	×	×		
8. Hold the drawing.											×		
9. Send out prizes, thank yous, and evaluate.											×	×	

13

Selling Goods

One fun way to raise money for your cause is by selling goods. These could be used items that you can sell in a garage sale, or goods that you create, like for a bake sale. There are variations of this strategy, including crafts fairs and Dine-to-Donate nights where a restaurant will donate a percentage of sales to a group's cause. In this chapter, we'll focus primarily on garage sales as an example and you can adapt this strategy in whatever way works best for you and your group.

Garage sales—also called tag sales, stoop sales, yard sales, or rummage sales—are popular because they epitomize the old adage that one person's trash is another person's treasure. It's hard to find anyone living in the United States who hasn't held one, bought something at one, or at the very least walked or driven by one. They are also easy to organize, and with a little extra time and planning, their fundraising potential can be increased by involving more people in the activity.

This chapter describes how to plan and organize an activity that focuses on selling donated items from as many people as you can manage. The sale can be held in someone's front yard, several neighbors' yards, or in a public setting, such as a community center or at an already planned event your group is having.

BEST USES

Selling goods doesn't require people who come to buy things to be committed to the cause you're raising money for. If you don't have a lot of prospects who you think would make contributions in response to a personal solicitation, or who would attend a house party or other event, you can still raise money through a sale. To raise more than a couple hundred dollars, however, consider getting several people involved and choosing a location that gets a lot of passersby.

THINGS TO CONSIDER

Selling goods can be organized in just a few weeks. However, plan on six to eight weeks' lead time if you want to recruit lots of people to help out and if you want to publicize the sale beyond your immediate neighborhood.

For garage sales, items to be sold should be in good condition, not broken or damaged things that are unlikely to sell easily. For sales of prepared food items, items should be properly wrapped and stored at their ideal temperature.

Think about where you'll store the donated items in the days (or weeks) leading up to the sale, and remember that you'll have to find some way to dispose of all of the unsold items at the end of the day. These considerations may cause you to limit the size of items you agree to accept for the sale.

COSTS

- Rental of place to hold the sale (if needed)
- Publicity
- Refreshments for volunteers
- Stickers for pricing items

STEPS TO TAKE

1. Make a plan.

2. Recruit volunteers.

3. Find a location to hold the sale.

4. Solicit donations of items to sell.

5. Publicize the sale.

6. Make final preparations.

7. Hold the sale.

8. Wrap up.

9. Evaluate and thank volunteers and people who donated items to sell.

As you go through the steps in detail, use the sample workplan at the end of the chapter to create a timeline and task list.

Step 1: Make a Plan

Set a goal for how much money you want to raise, then determine how many people you need to ask for donations. Assume that each person will donate enough items to bring in $50, on average. If, for example, you want to raise $1,000, then plan to have donations from at least twenty people. However, if even a few people have some big-ticket items such as kitchen items or small pieces of furniture in good condition, you won't need as many volunteers providing items to sell.

You'll also want to consider the ideal times people will be interested in the goods you're selling.

Step 2: Recruit Volunteers

Use the Volunteer Recruitment Form in Resource A to help identify potential volunteers. You'll be recruiting people for the following tasks:

- Find a location for the sale.

- Solicit and/or donate items for the sale.

- Arrange to have donated items picked up or dropped off.

- Store items ahead of time (if they can't be held at the sale location).

- Publicize the sale.

- Organize and price items; set up tables the morning of the sale.

- Serve as a cashier during the sale.

- Circulate and help customers; straighten up the sales tables throughout the day.

Step 3: Find a Location to Hold the Sale

Consider a location in your community that will draw a lot of impulse shoppers. If it's just you and a few neighbors organizing the sale, you can certainly hold it in your front yard or driveway. If it's something larger, you'll need a space that can accommodate the amount of stuff you sell that's also visible to passersby. The summer months, or any time of the year when people are out in the streets more, are the best times to hold a sale. If there's a risk of poor weather, look for an indoor space such as a community center, school gym, or church community room to hold the sale.

You can also add a sale to any existing event that your group is already planning, especially if you're selling food and refreshments. Another option could be joining an existing street fair, farmer's market, or other community event in your local area. Sometimes, these event organizers offer a free or reduced-price table fee for worthy causes.

Step 4: Solicit Donations of Items to Sell

Ask everyone you know to consider donating items to the sale. Ask them also to spread the word to people they know.

Give people examples of the kind of stuff you would like. For food sales, consider items that aren't too messy or hard to eat while standing. With a bake sale, this could be cookies, brownies, bars of various flavors, or cupcakes.

For garage sales, the best items are dishes, silverware, and other kitchen tools, and anything a student or person moving into a new home might need. Tools such as shovels, saws, hammers, and so on also sell well. Furniture, especially desks, chairs, sofas, and outdoor furniture in good shape, will sell if you advertise what you have. If you have things requiring electricity, such as toasters, microwave ovens, computers, and so on, make sure ahead of time that they work and note that on the item. It's also helpful to provide a way for someone to plug in the item and test it for themselves.

If you get donations of valuable items such as antiques, good furniture, or almost-new electronic equipment—anything that would sell for more than $100— you might want to look for other options for selling them that would bring in more money. This includes on an auction site or through an antique dealer or other reseller of big-ticket items. There are many instances of estate-sale experts finding rare books, high-end furniture, and even stamp or coin collections that are worth more by themselves than most of the other stuff put together.

Keep in mind the need to store the donated items before the sale. You'll be surprised at how much space they occupy in your closet or basement.

Step 5: Publicize the Sale

Although you're counting on some of your business coming from people who happen to walk or drive by, you'll get even more customers if people know about the sale ahead of time, especially those who may want to help your cause in addition to the possibility of getting some good bargains. This is arguably the most important step, as publicity is a large factor in this strategy's success. This step is also something that many volunteers can overlook because they get so caught up in event logistics.

Resource G on page 194 covers ways you can publicize your sale. As shown in the Sample Flyer, include in your publicity the kinds of items you have, such as "Infant and baby clothes and furniture," "Several almost complete sets of dishes," or "Everything a gardener could need."

GARAGE SALE
to benefit Restore Our River
Sat, April 17th
9:00 am - 3:00 pm
CLOTHING   BOOKS
TOYS   FURNITURE
at Lakeside Community Center
500 Main St

Step 6: Make Final Preparations

It's helpful to make yourself a checklist of things to do in the few days leading up to the sale. Here are some things to include:

- Get cash to make change and something to store it in. Be sure you have a calculator (which could be your phone).

- Set up with a fundraising platform to collect payments from credit cards and payment apps. Figure out where the money will be deposited (e.g., to your group's bank account if you have one, to an organization you know that is willing to handle it, or to your own personal bank account).

- For a garage sale, mark each item's price with a tag that will stay on and is easy to see. Price things slightly or well below their market value. The goal here is to get all the items sold. Profit in a garage sale is from volume.

- For a food sale, decide on the per-unit price for each unique item. Unlike a garage sale, generally there's minimal to no bartering in prepared food sales.

- Prepare signs to post at the sale to catch people's attention and to publicize that the sale is a fundraiser.

- Prepare a sign-in sheet for anyone who wants more information about your group (which is also a way to get new names for your newsletter).

- Make reminder calls to your volunteers.

- Have food and drink available for the volunteers.

Step 7: Hold the Sale

The following guidelines will help you have a successful sale:

- Have everything set up a half hour before your start time. For garage sales, the serious shoppers will already be at your sale by 7:30 or 8:00 A.M. Do *not* let anyone into the sale until you are open, no matter how much they beg and plead (and they will).

- As a reward for volunteering, you may want to let the volunteers have first dibs on items for sale either the night before or in the morning before the sale opens.

- Give volunteers a badge or a T-shirt with your group logo so buyers can easily identify who can answer questions.

- In a big sale, consider having volunteers stationed in a few places so they can keep an eye out on what's happening, as well as be available to answer any questions.

- Volunteers should continuously straighten things up and keep the sale site tidy and inviting.

- Two people should always stand by the cashbox, and every hour or so, one of them should take large bills and checks to a secure location.

- Authorize volunteers to lower the price of any single item by 10 percent and multiple items by 20 to 25 percent. At the halfway point, volunteers can lower the price of any single item by 20 percent and multiple items by 50 percent. At the end of the day, they can lower prices as much as they want to move everything out. For a garage sale where people try to bargain hard, the volunteer should stress that the sale is for a good cause and be willing to hold out for more money. Ideally, your volunteers are people who love garage sales themselves and so are familiar with the strategies buyers sometimes use—for example, insulting the items ("I would have thrown this in the trash," or "This is going to need a lot of work") or the pricing structure ("I have never seen prices like these. It's a tag sale, for heaven's sake."). You may want to have one volunteer authorized to make big deals, for example if someone offers to buy all the books you have.

- Offer to relieve volunteers after two or three hours, though some who love sales may be happy to stay all day. Most people will want to shift jobs so that they can look over all the items over the course of the day.

- Leave the place as clean or cleaner than when you arrived. Pick up all litter, and try not to fill the trash cans or dumpsters to the brim.

Step 8: Wrap Up

Because you're dealing with a lot of cash, it's best practice to have at least two people count the money and prepare the bank deposit. Ideally, you will deposit the money the same day. If that's not possible, lock the cash in a safe place until you can deposit it, but make sure that more than one person knows how much cash has been taken in.

Make arrangements to donate any leftover items in good condition to your local nonprofit thrift store. In some cases, they will come pick them up from you.

Step 9: Evaluate and Thank Volunteers and People Who Donated Items to Sell

If you think you may want to make this an annual event, jot down what worked well and what didn't, where the sale was held, how many volunteers were needed, how much money it raised, and anything else that might be helpful for someone else organizing such a sale for your group next year or in the future.

Thank everyone who donated items to the sale and who volunteered in any capacity.

The Bernal Heights Neighborhood Center Sale

The Bernal Heights Neighborhood Center (BHNC) in San Francisco has been holding a neighborhood-wide garage sale since 1992. The event is community led, with limited involvement of the BHNC staff. Neighbors are recruited to participate by holding a garage sale at their home on a designated day in August. Between 100 and 150 families sign up and pay a nominal $20 fee to participate and have their sale listed on a map of the event. Participants often donate some or all of the proceeds from their sales to BHNC, although it's not a requirement for participation. The center publicizes the event, puts together a map with the locations of the garage sales, and hosts its own garage sale for people who just want to donate a few items but not hold their own sale. The sale has become an enormous community event, with people coming from all over San Francisco and other nearby cities to shop for bargains. Although the income the event generates for the BHNC is relatively low—usually $4,000 to $5,000—the fact that it is led almost entirely by dedicated community volunteers has helped the BHNC strengthen its visibility in and relationship with the community and increase its presence in the neighborhood.

WORKPLAN

Workplan 13.1 on the following page summarizes the key steps necessary to implement this fundraising strategy and an estimated time frame for each step. It is meant to be a template from which to create your own plan and your own timeline. By taking the time to create a plan and timeline, you'll be more organized, more likely to avoid last-minute crises, and ultimately more successful in raising the money you need.

WORKPLAN 13.1
Selling Goods

WHAT	WHO	WHEN (WEEK WUMBER)							DONE
		1	2	3	4	5	6	7	
1. Make a plan.									
Set a fundraising goal and create a budget.		×							
Identify potential volunteer roles.		×							
2. Recruit volunteers.			×	×					
3. Find a location to hold the sale.				×					
4. Solicit donations of items to sell.			×	×	×	×	×		
Find a place to store items (before the sale).				×	×				
Arrange item dropoffs or pickups.				×	×	×	×		
5. Publicize the sale.					×	×	×		
6. Make final preparations.						×	×		
7. Hold the sale.							×		
8. Wrap up.							×		
9. Evaluate and send thank yous.								×	

14

Selling Services

There are many kinds of services that people pay for every day, from haircuts to car washes to yoga classes. Organizing a fundraising activity that recruits people with specific skills to offer those services free or at a reduced fee, with proceeds going to your cause, can be a very successful way to raise money.

The planning steps described in detail in this chapter are specifically for carrying out a car wash fundraiser, but we'll also briefly address how to adapt this idea for selling other services that people you know might be willing to donate for your cause.

The basic tasks associated with a car wash fundraiser are finding a location to hold the event and getting materials and volunteers to donate their time to wash the cars; the money you collect from washing cars is donated to your project or organization. If you know someone who has experience with car detailing, you can add waxing for an additional fee. Adding in other components, such as a bake sale or a raffle, can generate further income.

BEST USES

Selling services is a good choice if your volunteers are shy about asking for money directly and have something they're willing to provide free or at a discount to support the cause.

Think about popular services that people generally pay for and whether someone in your circle (or those of your volunteer team) might be willing to donate their skill to your group. Some things people commonly pay for and might be just as happy to have done by someone new, knowing that their payment is going to a good cause, include:

- haircuts,

- yard work,

- tax preparation,

- massage or other bodywork,

- foreign language class or coaching,

- computer tech support, and

- household repairs.

Organizing an activity focused on selling such services would be structured much like an auction but without the bidding. See Chapter 11, Silent and Virtual Auctions, to review the steps to carry out a successful sale of donated services.

These services can also be offered as an add-on at a community fundraiser. We've seen tattoo artists, tarot readers, and other fun, interactive service providers at beloved annual events.

Alternatively, you can ask those providing the services to donate a portion of their earnings from a specific day in exchange for the publicity they'll get from being part of your fundraising effort.

THINGS TO CONSIDER

For volunteers donating their skills, you want to consider how funds raised are directed to your group. The volunteer can collect and donate the proceeds, or the service recipient can provide a direct donation to your group.

For car washes, you need a location that has outdoor access to water and, because of the oils, toxic chemicals, and even the soap you wash the cars with, you'll need a method of safely disposing of the rinse water. Some communities restrict wastewater disposal, but even if yours doesn't, you don't want the water just running into the street, where it can pollute nearby water streams or sources. The location should also be able to accommodate several cars at once.

The information in this flyer from the City of Berkeley, California, provides some useful tips on safe disposal of wastewater from car wash fundraisers, so make sure to figure out this important issue in your planning process before deciding to hold a car wash.

Plan on having five to eight volunteers to wash the cars and a coordinator who deals directly with the customers and collects the money.

Car Wash Guidance
From the City of Berkeley, CA

Car washes have long been a favorite fundraiser for scout troops, schools, and other nonprofit groups. But in the last few years we have become aware of the negative impact car washes have on the environment. Dirty water containing soaps, detergent, residue from exhaust fumes, gasoline, and motor oil washes off the cars and directly into the storm drain, and then into the Bay. Collectively, car wash events can account for some serious pollution.

Choosing a Site

It is important to choose a site for your car wash where wastewater can be disposed of properly. Some popular sites, such as service stations and parking lots, usually do not have the necessary connections to the sanitary sewer system.

Here are some options:

❏ Find a sponsor for your car wash that uses a closed-loop washing system—one that recycles its water.

❏ Ask a local commercial car wash to donate part of their day's receipts or see if they will allow you to sell a special wash ticket.

❏ Hold your car wash at an industrial or commercial site that has a designated vehicle wash area.

❏ Rent a mobile washing system that can contain the water on the site. The collected water must be disposed of properly into the sanitary sewer, and not into a storm drain.

❏ Contact your city's local clean water program to see how you can set up an area to drain wash water to the sewer.

Weather is a major factor to consider when holding a car wash. Car washes work best in warmer months or climates and preferably when it's unlikely to rain.

One other consideration is whether you need liability insurance for car washes. One organization was sued by a customer who said his car was scratched at a benefit car wash. While this probably isn't a particularly common occurrence, it's worth finding out what the costs and requirements for insurance are in your community.

COSTS

- Supplies for what you're selling; for example, soap, brushes, drying cloths
- Refreshments for volunteers
- Materials for publicity

STEPS TO TAKE

1. Make a plan.
2. Recruit volunteers.
3. Find a location.
4. Set a date.
5. Publicize the sale.
6. Make final preparations.
7. Hold the sale.
8. Evaluate and thank the volunteers.

As you go through the steps in detail, use the sample workplan at the end of the chapter to create a timeline and task list.

Step 1: Make a Plan

Decide how much money you want to raise, how many volunteers you'll need, and for how many hours. For example, with a car wash, you'll want a location that can handle washing two cars at once, with at least two people washing each car. That means a total of four volunteers to wash the cars, a fifth person to direct people coming in to get their cars washed, and a sixth person to collect payment. If you charge $20 per car, and each wash takes fifteen minutes, you can wash eight cars per hour. For a day-long event (10 A.M. to 4 P.M.), you can wash as many as forty-eight cars, for a total of $960. Consider having three two-hour shifts. Decide if this will be a one-time event or repeated on several different days (say, every Saturday for one month).

You'll also need to figure out how you'll collect payments. You'll want to be able to accept both cash and online payments through payment apps. Most apps are available free of charge, and it's best to have a couple of the most popular options available so that customers don't have to download a new app to be able to pay for the service.

Step 2: Recruit Volunteers

Use Resource A, the Volunteer Recruitment Form (page 187), to identify potential volunteers. Here are the things you'll ask them to sign up for:

- Find a location for the sale.

- Conduct the service (wash cars, serve tables, etc.).

- Get the materials for the day (e.g., sponges, soap, buckets, chamois cloths for drying).

- Make signs.

- Make flyers to distribute around town during the week before the sale.

- Post the event in free publications and on local forums.

- Reach out to everyone they know publicizing the sale.

Step 3: Find a Location

Services can be sold at existing events. There can be a designated section or booth for someone to offer massages, tattoos, or tax accounting support.

Dine-to-donate nights are ideal at high-traffic restaurants and bars with sit-down service.

The best location for a car wash is on a busy street that has a lot of traffic going slowly enough that drivers have a chance to notice, slow down, and consider getting their car washed. Some groups have found a local gas station willing to let them set up a car wash on their premises. In that case, water for washing is available and you can approach people as they're pumping their gas. Otherwise, check with your local municipality about options for holding your car wash where you can manage safe wastewater disposal.

Step 4: Set a Date

Find a time that will maximize participation from volunteers and customers. Saturdays are usually the day people are most willing to get a massage or have their car washed. If you have enough people to help, consider running the sale over several weekends.

Step 5: Publicize the Sale

You'll get the most business if people know about it ahead of time and plan to come because, in addition to the service they seek, they want to help your cause. Resource G on page 194 covers ways you can publicize your sale. This is arguably the most important step, as publicity is a large factor in this strategy's success. This step is also something that many volunteers can overlook because they get so caught up in event logistics.

You can use the Sample Car Wash Flyer below as a template.

The $10 Car Wash Fundraiser

*An event to benefit the Campaign for Bilingual Education**

Saturday, May 28 | 9AM-3PM | Squeaky Clean Car Wash Parking Lot

Need your cars washed? Get it done all while supporting a great cause!

The Campaign for Bilingual Education (CBE) is working to develop more Spanish-language immersion programs in our public schools to provide native English- and Spanish-speaking students with conversational and reading skills in both languages.

Step 6: Make Final Preparations

There are a number of things to do to get prepared for the day of the sale:

- Get cash to make change and something to store it in.

- Set up a payment app to collect digital payments and figure out where the money will be deposited (e.g. to your group's bank account if you have one, to an organization you know that is willing to handle it, or to your own personal bank account).

- Prepare signs to hold up to catch the attention of passersby or to hang up if there's a place people walking or driving by will easily notice.

- Prepare a sign-up sheet for anyone who wants more information about your project and is interested in being on your newsletter list.

- Make reminder calls to your volunteers.

- Get materials—for car washes, this includes soap, sponges, scrubbers, and lots of towels to dry the cars and for volunteers to dry themselves off.

- Get refreshments for volunteers.

Step 7: Hold the Sale

If you plan to run the sale all day, schedule volunteers in two-hour shifts. Make it fun for them by providing food and drink and by rotating jobs.

Have someone available to talk to people who want more information about the project or the organization you're raising money for. Offer any literature you have and provide a sign-up sheet for anyone who wants to keep in touch about your work.

Step 8: Evaluate and Thank the Volunteers

If you think you may want to make this an annual event, jot down what worked well and what didn't, where the sale was held, how many volunteers were needed, how much money it raised, and anything else that might be helpful for someone else organizing such a sale for your group next year or in the future.

Thanking volunteers will make them more likely to volunteer again in the future.

Benefits

Benefits, a program for people recovering from substance misuse, held a weekly car wash on a busy street in Berkeley, California, for many years. As part of their community service requirement, the Benefits clients ran the car wash. They raised an average of $400 each week, which, over the course of the year, brought in close to $20,000 for the program.

A Car Wash Pledge Event

For many years, Diana Gomez, a music teacher at a public middle school in San Francisco, organized an annual, one-day-only car wash as a fundraiser for the school's music department. What made this car wash unusual—and financially very successful—is that it was done as a pledge-raising event, and the cars were washed for free. The students who were recruited to wash the cars asked people they knew to sponsor them for participating in the event. About 250 students participated each year. Each student was asked to get a minimum of $25 in pledges. There was a donation box for people whose cars were being washed to make a contribution. A bake sale was added to the event after a few years, which brought in additional funds. At the height of its success, the car wash raised $12,000 from the pledges, another $1,000 in donations from people whose cars were washed, and $300 to $500 from the bake sale.

WORKPLAN

Workplan 14.1 on the following page summarizes the key steps necessary to implement this fundraising strategy and an estimated time frame for each step. It is meant to be a template from which to create your own plan and your own timeline. By taking the time to create a plan and timeline, you'll be more organized, more likely to avoid last-minute crises, and ultimately more successful in raising the money you need.

WORKPLAN 14.1
Selling Services

WHAT	WHO	WHEN (WEEK NUMBER)						DONE
		1	2	3	4	5	6	
1. Make a plan.		×						
Identify potential volunteer roles.		×						
2. Recruit volunteers.		×	×					
3. Find a location.		×						
4. Set a date.			×					
5. Publicize the sale/activity.				×	×	×		
6. Make final preparations.					×	×		
Make reminder calls to volunteers.					×	×		
7. Hold the sale/activity.						×		
8. Evaluate and thank the volunteers.							×	

CONCLUSION

We hope that by now you're excited to try one or more of the fundraising strategies described in this book. We hope, too, that you can see that fundraising is by its nature a community-building activity that not only brings in much-needed cash for the causes we believe in, but also expands the networks of people who learn about important social or neighborhood issues and join in making a difference in the world. Your work deserves the financial support you can round up—whether you're planting trees, stopping toxic waste dumping, advocating for racial justice in your school or workplace, working to end gun violence, or organizing recreational programs for kids. The information provided here about how to carry out a diverse range of fundraising activities is based on the real-life experiences of thousands of people, projects, and organizations throughout the United States. Following the instructions in this book, you can join them in creating your dream of a better world.

We wish you great fundraising success, and fun in getting there!

RESOURCES

A. VOLUNTEER RECRUITMENT FORM

Use this worksheet to identify potential volunteers for your fundraising project.

NAME	EMAIL	PHONE	ADDRESS	RELATIONSHIP TO YOU OR THE GROUP	WHAT WILL YOU ASK THEM TO DO?[1]	DATE OF RECRUITMENT CALL OR EMAIL	RESPONSE TO RECRUITMENT CALL OR EMAIL	SKILLS AND EXPERIENCE[2]

1 Refer to the chapter that describes the strategy you'll be carrying out. Each description includes a list of tasks that you'll want to recruit volunteers to help out with. Use that list to come up with items for this column.

2 Use this column for relevant information about this person: language skills, experience (such as graphic design, fundraising, or computer skills), and so on.

B. WHO CAN YOU ASK?

If you're having a hard time coming up with a list of people to ask to support your project, here are some ideas to get you going. You may be surprised at how many people you know and how many are willing to give money to a good cause.

❏ **Family:** Parents, grandparents, kids, siblings, aunts, uncles, cousins, and in-laws.

❏ **Friends:** Your friends, friends of your friends, and friends of your spouse or partner.

❏ **Social acquaintances:** Old friends you see only on occasion, friends from college or school, your former professors or teachers, friends from your old job, and people from the hotline or community group where you used to volunteer.

❏ **Neighbors:** From next door, upstairs, downstairs, down the hall, the whole building! People you always run into when you go jogging or walk the dog; people you see at the grocery store; your co-op board, tenants' association, landlord, tenants, or superintendent; your babysitter or childcare collective; your carpool; and the parents of your children's friends.

❏ **People from your house of worship:** Your religious leader, members of the congregation, and people you share holidays with.

❏ **Colleagues:** People at your workplace; your current and former partners, clients, and supervisors; people who used to work in the office but recently left; colleagues from community work; union leaders and activists, your steward, your business agent, and other union staff.

❏ **Club members:** From your block association, political club, book club, food co-op, local peace or environmental group, the PTA, your local school board, civic organizations, and your community board.

❏ **Leisure contacts:** Members of your bowling league, volleyball team, cooking group, pickup basketball crowd; the bridge club; your poker buddies; other students in night school or yoga class; fellow gym-goers; people you've met on beach or camping trips; people you sing with in a choir, jam with, or go caroling with; dance partners; and people you walk with, garden with, and vacation with.

❏ **Professionals and service providers:** Your barber or hairstylist, lawyer, dentist, doctor, chiropractor, pharmacist, broker, butcher, dry cleaner, or baker; repairperson or handyperson; your house cleaner, lawn service, pool service, or heating and cooling maintenance crew; and your mechanic.

❏ **People on past lists:** The invitation list to your last party; your holiday card list; the program from your last reunion; and your professional and personal contact lists.

C. TIPS ON ASKING INDIVIDUALS FOR MONEY

When you remember that people like to give money to causes they care about, you might be a little less nervous to ask them for support. If you're asking someone you know who also believes in the cause, they're very likely to say yes, or at least be nice about saying no. Here are some tips on getting comfortable with asking for money:

❏ Prepare a list of people you would like to ask, using Resource B, and start with the people you feel most confident about or are most comfortable approaching. Go to the ones you are more hesitant about after you've had a little practice (and some success).

❏ Practice first with a friend.

❏ Ask for a specific amount of money or at least the range of gifts you're looking for.

❏ Be prepared to talk about why this cause is important to you. People like to hear about your personal relationship to the cause; they become inspired by your enthusiasm.

❏ Be open to any questions your potential supporters may have, and take an interest in what they care about.

❏ Don't worry about being able to answer every question a prospect may have. You can always tell them that you'll find out and get back to them with the answer.

❏ After you ask, stop talking! Wait for the person to respond. They may respond with a question or they may have to think about it, but don't assume you know what they're going to say.

❏ If they say yes, make a plan for how they're going to make the donation.

❏ Always thank your prospects whether they give or not (for taking the time to think about it, for giving, for supporting you in whatever way they can).

D. TIPS FOR MAKING A PITCH AT AN EVENT

At a house party, community fundraiser, or other public event, the pitch for donations is a very important part of the program.

But pitches aren't limited to fundraising events. Got an already scheduled training, meeting, or gathering with your group? Add a fundraising pitch at the end of it. It can be as simple as stating why your group's work is important, sharing what funds will be raised for, and passing a bucket around to collect cash and checks, as well as giving an online donation option.

The following tips will help prepare you for that crucial moment.

❏ **Choose your moment.** Time the pitch so that the most people will be there to hear it and so it occurs at the point of highest energy in the program.

❏ **Keep it short and simple.** Your pitch will be more powerful if you are confident, speak from the heart, and keep it brief.

❏ **Dramatize.** Remind people what's at stake.

❏ **Be creative about the ask**. See the Sample Pitch Language section below for ideas.

❏ **Lead by example.** Have "plants" who will pull out their form of payment and declare the gift they're making (if part of the program) or begin making their contribution as people come forward.

❏ **Make it easy.** Pass collection baskets for cash. Have at least one volunteer stationed with a way to give by credit card; this could be a laptop with the donation page up and ready or a credit card reader phone attachment. Have at least one volunteer stationed to hand out an envelope, donation card, or slip and a pen to every person who would like to donate by check and to answer any questions about making the check out. Consider if and how you can take donations from mobile payment apps.

❏ **Collect the money.** Have a team of people politely but actively collect cash and checks shortly after the pitch. Collectors should hold baskets as they approach people, not just leave the basket on a table or even just pass it around. They should make sure to approach, make eye contact with, and thank everyone. Have at least one volunteer with a basket and another volunteer who can process credit card payments stand at the door to catch every attendee as they leave.

Sample Pitch Language

Start with why this cause is important to you, as personally as possible. "When I learned that a close friend of mine was dealing with an opioid addiction, thanks to the overprescribing of painkillers, I felt I had to do something. Not only was it heartbreaking to see her struggling like this, but I knew that there are hundreds if not thousands of people just like her in our community."

Visioning exercise. "Close your eyes and picture." Paint a vision of hope for the possibility of change in our community. Use humor—ask your audience to envision the project's work, then envision raising their hand and reaching into their pocket or purse to get their checkbook. Ask them to envision writing their lucky number, then adding lots of zeroes to it.

Double what you came here to give. "If you came here thinking you would give $20, consider giving $40. If you came here to give $50, consider $100."

Challenge people to meet the goal. State the fundraising goal for the party and ask people to help you meet it. "Tonight we're trying to raise $5,000. How much can you give toward that goal?" Report back on how much you have raised and ask if people will pitch in more if you need just a little more to reach the goal. Celebrate when you reach the goal.

Lead with a gift. The person doing the pitch can lead with their own gift: "I'm going to start off the night with a gift of (so many dollars)." It's especially powerful for the host of a house party to share to inspire their guests to give an ambitious amount.

Have people announce their gifts. While this isn't something everyone will want to do or feel is appropriate for their community, it can be a powerful motivator to others in the room. Ask people to stand up or raise their hands if they can give $500, $200, $100, $50, $25, or $5. Clap and cheer as enthusiastically for the $5 contributions as you do for the $500 contributions—each contribution is important in helping you reach your total! You can ask a couple of attendees ahead of time to get it started and keep the momentum going.

Ask people to stretch. Ask people to contribute what is significant for them: "The issue is important, and that is why you are all here with us. I would like to ask you to think about why you care about this cause, and then make the biggest contribution you can, one that is truly meaningful for you. Is it the equivalent of a mortgage payment or a car payment? If that's too much, can you forgo a dinner out each month and make a monthly contribution?"

A Final Note about the Pitch

The person making the pitch has to be comfortable with what they're asking people to do, so if encouraging larger gifts (e.g., "Double what you had in mind" or "Add some zeroes to the amount you were considering") feels like too much, there's no need for them to do that. Speaking from the heart, from their own relationship to the cause and about what they're willing to do themselves, is ultimately the most important.

E. VOLUNTEER TRACKING SHEET

NAME	EMAIL	PHONE NUMBER	ADDRESS	ROLE THEY PLAYED	HOW THEY WANT TO STAY INVOLVED	THANKED?

F. IDEAS FOR AUCTION ITEMS AND/OR RAFFLE PRIZES TO SOLICIT

When brainstorming items to solicit, remember to ask your team of volunteers what they can offer, as well as who they know that might be able to contribute something. Think, too, about whom your group does business with and whether they might be a potential source of an auction item or raffle prize. Here are some ideas.

Gift cards from local retailers:

❏ Bookstores

❏ Sporting goods stores

❏ Clothing stores

❏ Restaurants

❏ Movie theaters

Services:

❏ Massages

❏ Haircuts

❏ Home-cooked dinner

❏ Dog walking

Vacations:

❏ Airline tickets

❏ Frequent-flyer miles

❏ Night at an inn or bed and breakfast

Classes or personalized instruction:

❏ Foreign-language instruction

❏ Music lessons

❏ Knitting, sewing, or gardening

❏ Self-defense

❏ Yoga, tai chi

Other things people like:

❏ Basket of skin care products or small food items

❏ Home-baked cakes, cookies, or pies

❏ Cash

G. PUBLICIZING YOUR PUBLIC EVENT

For your event to be successful in meeting your goals, you'll want to publicize it to people both within and outside of your group's immediate networks. Here are some ideas to get you started.

❏ Create an invitation, which can be digital only or, if you'd like, a print version to mail out.

❏ Ask volunteers to send the invitation emails and texts about the event to everyone they know.

❏ Share about the event in your newsletter and on social media.

❏ Create and post flyers in neighborhood businesses, in the communities you work in, and with organizations you know.

❏ Post in online neighborhood forums.

❏ Take out inexpensive or free ads in community papers.

❏ Get a public service announcement (PSA) on your local radio station.

H. SPONSORSHIPS

Sponsorships are donations made primarily by businesses, but also sometimes by individuals, in support of an organization's event or a specific project. Generally, events do not make money through ticket sales alone because the cost of putting on an event makes the "profit margin" very small or sometimes nonexistent. This is why sponsorships can be the difference between meeting your fundraising goal or not when you're producing an event. The pitch to potential sponsors is that they will be publicly acknowledged in event materials and at the event itself with their names listed on the invitation and in any program materials or displays at the event.

When you're holding an event that includes a meal, another form of sponsorship is to ask businesses and individuals to purchase an entire table (usually eight to ten tickets). Organizations or individuals who agree to sponsor a table pay a lump sum—usually more than the actual cost of the total number of seats at the table—and then give (or share the cost of) tickets to people within their organization or to friends.

Sponsorships also offer an opportunity to reach a wider audience, as sponsors will sometimes promote the event to their own networks. Sponsorships can potentially lead to long-term partnerships with local businesses. Securing sponsorships from allied nonprofits and well-respected businesses can enhance your group's visibility and credibility within the community.

Depending on your project, you may need to think through which businesses might be appropriate sponsors and which ones would hurt your organization's image. For example, if you are working on environmental issues, sponsorship by a company known to pollute the air in your community would likely alienate your supporters. On the other hand, some businesses may genuinely support your cause, and it might be smart for everyone to let them enhance their image and for you to receive some much-needed funds. If you're part of an LGBTQ group, a local queer bar could support your event with recruitment in addition to monetary and in-kind support.

You may want to consider different levels of sponsorship and corresponding benefits for each level. Because business sponsors will want something in exchange for their support—publicity for their business, at the very least—having more benefits for larger donations can be helpful. Here's an example of what sponsors could get for different levels of support:

Level 1: Organizer's Circle ($250)

❏ Recognition on the event website and social media

❏ Logo placement on the event program and signage

❏ Two complimentary event tickets

Level 2: Movement Builder ($500)

❏ All benefits from Organizer's Circle level

❏ A table for eight guests at the event

❏ Recognition during the event program

Level 3: Champion of Change ($1,000)

❏ All benefits from Movement Builder level

❏ Pre-event reception with keynote speaker

❏ Full-page ad in event program

❏ Recognition on all event marketing materials (print and digital)

Here is a sample letter you can adapt when soliciting businesses and individuals to sponsor your event:

Dear [Business Name],

I hope this message finds you well. I'm writing to ask for your support for a project to raise awareness of the problem of gun violence in our community and to promote a "Violence-Free Neighborhood" initiative.

We're organizing a community event, featuring music, spoken word, and a dessert buffet on May 10th and are hoping to raise $10,000 (after expenses). We hope to get one hundred people to the event, and hundreds more will learn about it, and about our generous sponsors, through the publicity we'll be carrying out.

With the help of businesses like [Business Name], who are known to support critical community causes and needs, we are confident we can meet our goal.

We are reaching out to invite [Business Name] to become a sponsor for this event. Sponsorship presents a unique opportunity to showcase your commitment to our community while gaining visibility among our diverse audience.

As a sponsor, depending on the level you choose, your business would receive a variety of benefits, including logo placement on event materials, recognition on our website and social media platforms, and opportunities for on-site branding.

Attached, you will find a detailed sponsorship packet outlining the various levels of support and their associated benefits. We would be delighted to discuss how we can partner with you to make a meaningful impact. Please feel free to reach out to me directly at [phone number] or [email address] to schedule a time to connect.

Thank you for considering this opportunity to collaborate with Violence-Free Neighborhood Initiative.

Warm regards,

ACKNOWLEDGMENTS

This book is the result of much collaboration, which is fitting for a work that stresses the importance of people coming together to make a difference with their time and their money. Many of the fundraising strategies we describe here were originally written about by others. We adapted them to provide a greater level of detail and how-to for readers who are primarily volunteers carrying out these fundraising strategies in their free time.

The original idea for the first edition of this book came from Johanna Vondeling, Stephanie's editor at Jossey-Bass. Johanna convinced us that this book needed to be written and that, while there are many books on fundraising, few are written explicitly for volunteers, community members, and activists. Johanna continued her support nearly two decades later when Stephanie approached her for advice about doing a new edition. We thank Johanna for her insights, advice, and connections to others in the publishing world, including our "book sherpa," Maureen Forys. In addition to helping us navigate the world of self-publishing, through the many unexpected hurdles and hoops required, Maureen did a fabulous job designing the book—not an easy task with the variety of graphic elements we wanted to include.

A huge shoutout goes to Priscilla Hung, one of four amazing fundraisers who read and provided invaluable feedback on the first draft of the book. Priscilla graciously allowed us to use some of her writing, which we incorporated into several chapters in this book. In addition, Chanelle Gallant, Kim Klein, and Ambar Pinto, all of them fundraisers (among their other many talents), read the first draft of our manuscript and gave invaluable feedback, without which this book would not have been nearly as useful or relevant.

Our thanks also go to the many organizations and people we've worked with over the years who have put these ideas and more to work raising money for great causes. They were an inspiration and a reminder that fundraising really can be done in all kinds of communities by all kinds of people.

FROM HALEY

Not all of us are fortunate enough to directly collaborate with and learn from our mentors, and each day working on this book has given me gratitude for the wisdom my coauthor Stephanie Roth imparted to me through our time sharing stories, conducting generative debates (Are physical flyers still relevant for event turnout? How do people generally pay for items at a garage sale?), and walking through the start-to-finish process of dusting off a twenty-year-old book to adapt it to the current era.

My entrance into fundraising, like many people's and in honor of this title, was accidental. I was a software engineer in the Bay Area who thought fundraising for social justice causes from tech worker friends could be something fun to try. To get started, I immediately bought and fell in love with *The Accidental Fundraiser*, and it demystified the process so I could make a list of people, develop my pitch, and start sending out emails and texts to schedule one-on-ones.

From this book, I was able to colead Showing Up Racial Justice Bay Area's fundraising committee (lovingly known as FunCom) to raise $25,000 in one month entirely through volunteer efforts. To FunCom leaders, including but not limited to Elliot Karl, Josie Ahrens, Ari Turrentine, Judy Grether, Rose Mendelsohn, Heather Buchheim, Leah Olm: thank you for teaching me how fundraising can and should be integrated into every possible organizing opportunity from trainings to rallies to mass meetings.

Many years later, I founded an organization focused on building the base and resources of social movements through training and coaching volunteer fundraisers. Donor Organizer Hub's formation and adaptation have been possible due to the advice, soundboarding, and wisdom of Mario Lugay and Lisa Tracy. Thank you for opening up my mind to different ways that donations are an invitation to our movements and how we can build leadership ladders for donors.

And though he cringed at my suggestion of acknowledging him in this section, all of the appreciation and love goes to my spouse, Danny Henn. Thank you for all the listening, soundboarding, feeding me and the cats, and reminding me to go to bed during the busiest times in book writing. Thank you for encouraging me to say yes to the once-in-a-lifetime opportunity to write a new edition of the book that made me a fundraiser with the person who has become a dear mentor, friend, and colleague. We've had twelve years of cross-country distance, graduations, moves, job changes, deaths, and marriage, and now let's add a book to the list!

FROM STEPHANIE

I want to thank my colleague and friend, Haley Bash, who convinced me that this book deserved a second edition and offered to take the lead in updating the content to reflect changes in the world of grassroots, volunteer-led fundraising practices. Haley was a true partner in this endeavor, always showing up with a positive attitude, even when we faced stressful moments of time crunches or disagreements. This meant a lot to me! I always love learning new things, even at my advanced age, and I learned a lot from Haley during the process of writing this book.

My colleagues and friends at Klein & Roth Consulting (Rona Fernandez, Nancy Otto, and Stan Yogi, as well as my partner in life and work, Kim Klein) deserve much credit for deepening my understanding of social justice fundraising, especially with a racial and economic justice lens. We worked together as a team for over a decade (and for some of us, over twenty years), supporting each other with our client work, through huge personal losses and also personal joy and accomplishment.

I've worked with many organizations over the past four decades and learned from all of them, but I want to give a special appreciation to my team of volunteers fundraisers at CLAM (Community Land Trust of West Marin), with whom I worked from 2017 to 2022 and who demonstrated and affirmed the power of volunteer leadership in raising money. Myn Adess, Susan Brayton, Christa Burgoyne, Maureen Cornelia, Corey Ohama, Nancy Vahinger, and Elvira Xaxni were phenomenal volunteer leaders in the organization who demonstrated the importance of relationships in building strong and meaningful community support for a cause. The board and volunteers of CLAM were responsible for raising the lion's share of the budget for the organization before, during, and after my time on staff.

And finally, I thank my wife, Kim Klein, for her constant encouragement and good humor, especially in those moments when I was overwhelmed by this and other projects. In addition to learning much about fundraising from her over the years, she's taught me a lot about the importance of making sure that everyone can see themselves in community and social change work, which in part means speaking plainly and without jargon. Her significant contributions to the body of knowledge in fundraising are well known, and many of them inform the perspective of this book. More important to me than all of that is her love and support over the past thirty-six years.

THE AUTHORS

Haley Bash (they/she) is a grassroots fundraiser, distributed organizer, and facilitator with 15 plus years of experience in the social movement sector. They are the founder and executive director of Donor Organizer Hub, a launchpad and community for people who fundraise for movement causes from their networks. Haley scaled The States Project's giving circle community and launched Showing Up for Racial Justice Bay Area's peer-to-peer fundraising program. Haley previously built the largest volunteer-run texting program for down-ballot candidates at Red2Blue Texting. They are a fundraising coach with Transgender Strategy Center and serve on the Steering Committee of the Grassroots Fundraising Network. They live in Oakland, California, with their spouse and two cats.

Stephanie Roth (she/her) has been a trainer, consultant, and coach with a focus on fundraising, board development, and meeting facilitation for organizations working for social justice for over thirty years. Most recently, she served as development director at the Community Land Trust of West Marin from 2017 to 2022. She has served on many boards, including of Jewish Voice for Peace, where she continues to be an active member, and where she helped launch their successful grassroots fundraising program in 2002.

Stephanie has trained and written widely on the topic of fundraising and organizational development, including as editor of the *Grassroots Fundraising Journal*. She lives in Berkeley, California, with her wife and their two cats.